From Scared to Sacred

Lessons in Learning to Dance with Life

Carol Woodliff

For rights information contact: info@carolwoodliff.com

Cover Illustration by Annie b. www.annieb-art.co.uk

Back cover photograph by Janell Mithani

ISBN-13: 978-0-9856571-0-9

Inspiration, Spirituality, Memoir

Dedicated to Mom & Dad, my first spiritual teachers, thank you for supporting me in life and from the great beyond. You are always in my heart.

CONTENTS

YOU WANT ME TO DO *WHAT?*

Have you ever felt like life was a test and you were flunking? I have for most of my life. While to a good portion of the world I looked like I had it together, it was all an act covering up layer after layer of insecurities and fears. Inside me was a deep-seated story that I wasn't enough, that I wasn't doing it right.

I had a sense that I was sent to Earth with an important mission to do big things. Problem was, somewhere along the way of incarnating in a body, I forgot what my mission was. That's how this book begins, with that overwhelming feeling that I was blowing it and going to flunk the test. I was 47 and still searching. The need to figure it out soon was overwhelming me. You could call it a mid-life crisis, or a dark night of the soul moment, but I felt the clock ticking.

It was April 2008, and I was a hypnotherapist and speaker. I loved working with my clients and being in front of groups. Financially, I wasn't quite the success I had hoped to be. I was working a part-time job as a paralegal to fill in the gaps in my income. But it wasn't just about money. That nagging feeling that I was missing something wouldn't go away.

Was I in the wrong career? Was I supposed to be speaking about something other than stress management and goal setting? Should I go back to school? Move to a different city? Move to another country? Was it because I wasn't in a relationship? I was single with no children. This wasn't how I thought my life would be, but here I was. With no husband or children to consider, I had the freedom to change my life, but I didn't know what to do to fix the nagging feeling that something wasn't right. At the same time I felt guilty for wanting more because I knew in comparison to so many others, my life was blessed.

After attending yet another workshop on how to invigorate my business, where this latest business guru's method felt more like a pyramid scheme than the answers to my search, I was fed up. What was I doing wrong? I felt like I had more to offer than the business guru. I didn't want his career, or his system. I knew I was supposed to be doing something else but I didn't know what that something was.

Everyone tells you the answers lie within but I had been searching for answers for so long, I was tired and feeling quite cranky and hopeless. Where were my answers? Where was my stuff? I wanted to earn my living with integrity from my heart and I wanted a comfortable existence too. Was that too much to ask?

So many questions were racing through my mind. I decided that it might help if I wrote my thoughts down on paper. I put on some soothing Native American flute meditation music and sat down in my big white overstuffed chair in the corner of the living room of my small cottage with my journal by my side and Sadie, my sweet canine companion sleeping at my feet. I closed my eyes and listened to the music and the wanderings of my mind for about fifteen minutes. Questions bubbled up expressing my longing for answers: "What am I missing? What is it you have to say to me? Is there something I'm supposed to learn?" Like a child throwing a tantrum, I threw up my hands and petulantly asked the Universe, "WHAT? What do you want me to *do?*" The energy was too much to contain in a quiet meditative state. I opened my eyes and the journal and began to write. My hand flew across the page as I wrote about those hopes, fears and doubts, but after several minutes something shifted and another "voice" took over, and The Voice said:

> *Listen and don't judge. Sit and write and let me flow through you. I have many books to write, many stories to tell, many miracles to perform. And I want to use you. Are you willing to step aside from smallness and let me use you? Are you? Will you commit to be with me an hour every day to take down the messages? Will you be with me?*

Chills ran up and down my spine as I thought, "You want me to do *what? Miracles?* You've got to be kidding me!" I called one of my best friends, Karen, and read her the message. She calmly said, "I guess you don't have a choice, you have to write then, don't you?" She didn't call the men in white coats and for that I will always be grateful. For several months that is what I did. I made time each day to listen and write down what I heard without editing or second-guessing. There on the page my doubts and fears were answered by poetic words of wisdom that touched me deeply.

A few days into my writing commitment, I had already filled a journal. Although the things that were flowing through me were beautiful, I didn't trust them. So I wrote in a new journal, "I'm scared," but when I looked down I had actually written "I'm sacred." I tried again. "I'm scared" and once again I looked down and it said, "I'm sacred." "Funny," I thought to myself, "it is only two letters turned around but look at the difference. What is *that* about? Why can't I write the word 'scared'?" I asked. The Voice replied, *"Ah! You are finally getting it — that is the journey from scared to sacred. You think you are scared but you are not. You may feel scared but you are sacred, and I want you to explore fully your sacredness."*

I kept repeating those four words "From Scared to Sacred." They felt welcoming. I was intrigued, "What would it be like to actually feel sacred?" At the same time I wondered how this could be happening to me. I have always been the practical one — the one you go to when you want to get something done. I wasn't one of those *woo-woo* ladies with a beaded caftan and incense who channeled guides from another dimension. (No offense if you are!)

Where was This Voice coming from? Was I having a spiritual experience or was my imagination working overtime? If it was me, it wasn't a "me" I had spent much time with in the past. Was it my guardian angel, a spirit guide or God? Was this how Moses felt at the burning bush? I wasn't egotistical enough to compare myself to Moses, was I? I hoped I wasn't going to have to do something like lead people out of Egypt—forty years wandering in the desert wasn't my idea of a good time!

Every time I asked The Voice who it was, it gave me a version of "I am" in its answer. "I am the highest love." "I am the deepest knowing in all knowing." Sounded a lot like the names of God, and yet claiming to hear God sounded dangerous and a little arrogant to me. The words and energies that flowed through me as I wrote were so beautiful they often made me cry. It was as though the highest love was pouring forth and a dear friend was taking my hand. I didn't want to get so caught up in trying to name the voice that I missed the messages. So I settled on simply calling it "The Voice" as I wrote. But I also described it to myself as The Sacred, The Divine, The Universe, Spirit, The God Voice and sometimes My Inner Guru.

A friend of mine, who is a judge, jokingly asked me, "The Voice isn't telling you to drink your urine or kill people or hurt yourself, is it?" Thankfully I was able to reply "No, no and no." As a judge, she hears the stories of people who claim to hear voices at their psychiatric commitment hearings. My thoughts flashed to the skinny homeless lady with the stringy long graying hair and rotting teeth who used to live near my college apartment. She would call out, "God is damning you to hell, you slut!" as I tried not to catch her eye. I knew her message wasn't personal; she repeated it to every woman who walked by. Curse Lady, as we called her, needed psychological help. My Voice wasn't judging other people or telling me to hurt myself. It was encouraging me to be more loving and accepting.

I wondered, "Why me?" I wasn't one of those enlightened, saintly souls who loved to meditate, who traveled to exotic places like India, or were ultra-religious and so committed to living in spirit that they became monks or nuns. My story was that these types of events didn't happen to people like me; they only happened to other people. But they were happening, weren't they? The teachings were so loving and perfect for my life that they gave me goose bumps. If they hadn't affected me that way, I might have been able to discount the experience as a fantasy and move on. I tried. I would avoid my journal for days, but then something would call me back and every time I returned I would realize what a gift the experience was.

After eight weeks, I had filled several journals. When I read back what I had written, it read something like this: Carol complaining and whining; Carol asking questions; more whining; The Voice with a message; more doubting; another message, and so on. Beautiful messages popped out amid lots of junk. Those messages open each chapter of this book. It is one thing to have all those lovely poetic teachings and completely another thing to know what to do with them.

The contrast between those messages and my day-to-day life made me laugh. I was having an experience that I jokingly called being "spiritually bipolar." I'd feel vibrantly alive when I read those messages, like I was a surfer catching that perfect wave of love; then I'd go back to the tasks of my day-to-day life and find that I felt like I was being sucked under, thrown down to the bottom of the ocean and slammed into the rocks. How could I be so in tune one minute and so lost the next? All I could do was shrug off my "wipe out" and show up at the page again. The essays that form the second part of each chapter were my way of examining those messages in relationship to the experiences of my own life to demonstrate to myself that it was possible to live them.

Writing was a process that felt like home to me. I wrote stories when I was a child. I majored in journalism. I've written plays and have helped others edit their books. When I write, there are times I slip into a creative stream. When that inspiration is flowing, I have learned to appreciate the gift. But this inspiration was different. Something was pushing me to listen and reflect in a much bigger way than I ever had before. In the struggle to write about what each passage meant to me, I shifted and grew.

The difference between the words *scared* and *sacred* is a small change in how you write or type the word. The changes that move us from scared to sacred in life are small shifts in perspective. But small shifts are not necessarily easy shifts. How many of us can name exactly what we need to shift but are still clueless about how to shift the energy that keeps us stuck in the old story?

I would have preferred to keep my humanness and personal stories to myself. But the book that was demanded of me by this experience won't allow me to claim "expert" status. I am not a guru, but a fellow traveler on this journey we call life. While I've had an amazing experience that has brought me closer to the sacred within, I don't pretend to have all the answers for myself, much less for you. I'm in the process of discovery. My hope is that the adage that the personal is universal is true and that by sharing my stories, you will be inspired to take your own journey of discovering the knowing inside you. Those whispers speak with a resonance so deep that you know they are true. They are quiet, strong, certain and loving. They are the truths felt in your heart that give you wings.

But I'm getting ahead of myself. In the beginning it was all about learning to be with my fears. . . .

CHAPTER 1

FEAR IS NOT THE ENEMY

Fear is not an enemy to be destroyed. It is a messenger to greet and discern the wisdom of its messages. To grow, learn how to dance with fear not fight it. Be gentle and compassionate; hold your fear like a child. Listen. What is it trying to tell you? Is it truly telling you to do something for your physical safety or is it keeping you from living? Only when you can discern this difference, will you transform.

Whatever fear or burden you carry, there is a home for you. There is a place to rest. There are open arms to hold you and there is a fire of love so strong to warm you. When you are scared, turn the fear over to me. Ask me to send love, guidance and protection. I hear you. I surround you with angel wings. I carry you to love until you remember it inside. I hold it for you. I hold the vision for you bright and clear. I am near. When you call upon me, I am there in ways only the heart can see — perfect moments of synchronicity, helpful friends and strangers, moments of inspiration and love.

More love than your simple heart can hold. I am there. Breathe and fall back into my arms. I will catch you and raise you up when fear overtakes you. I will catch you and cradle you when you are sad. I am pure light and love and I am always yours. This moment till the end of time, I am yours, Love. Love is always yours. I will hold you until you remember.

~~~

"We gain strength, and courage, and confidence by each experience in which we really stop to look fear in the face . . . we must do that which we think we cannot." — Eleanor Roosevelt

~~~

June 2008. I have been taking down messages from The Voice for two months now. I am sitting at a picnic table with my journal eating a turkey submarine sandwich on a humid summer day in a small park in Rockford, Illinois, the town I grew up in. The white and puffy clouds are a welcome break from the thundershowers that have been pounding the area for days causing widespread flooding. I am glad to be out in the sunshine even though it is sticky and my t-shirt clings to my back. The light breeze that stirs the leaves of the tall maple trees nearby does nothing to dry my skin, as the air is almost saturated with moisture.

I hear a small, pure voice call out "Mommy, Mommy! I'm scared Mommy!" It is panicked enough that I look to see its source—a little girl about five years old with dark curly hair in pigtails and big brown eyes, pink shirt, blue shorts and sneakers. She is on the monkey bars in the playground area. She has lost her forward momentum and is just hanging there unable to move, afraid to let go with one arm and reach for the next rung, afraid to drop to the ground.

Her mother, a 30-something woman with brown hair cut short into a crown of curls, has been pushing her brother in a baby swing. Mom hurries over, catches the little girl around the middle in a big hug and gently lowers her to the ground. With a quick kiss on the top of her head and an encouraging smile, Mom returns to the adorable baby slumped in the swing. I watch as the girl eyes the monkey bars, rubs her hands against her shorts, and climbs the side ladder with determination. "You can do it," her mom yells out as the little girl swings from one rung to the other. "Keep moving. Don't stop!"

After several more tries with Mom rescuing her each time, the little girl finally swings easily across to the very end. On the ground, the pigtails bob as she jumps up and down to celebrate while Mom and I applaud.

Part of me longs for those days where the things I feared could be easily dealt with by a hug from my mommy or daddy. Even in my adult years I could take risks because I had my family as backup. "If this doesn't work, the worst that can happen is: I'll have to move back home," I said as I left my full-time job to pursue acting. I valued my independence but that safe harbor was there. Now there was no moving back with Mom. It was my turn to help her.

Mom was 87 and lived in an assisted care home due to a stroke and Parkinson's disease that limited her mobility and ability to live safely alone. I knew she was scared and I lived 1700 miles away. My visits were not frequent enough. My career choices had made traveling back more often financially difficult. Mom's speech had been affected by her illnesses so phone time was frustrating for her. It could take a long time for her to express a thought. My sister, Luanne, bore the burden of overseeing Mom's day-to-day care. I felt inadequate as I saw Mom's life slipping away.

My mind kept telling me that I needed to be responsible. Should I move to Illinois and get a "real" job to be closer to Mom? The Voice was giving me lovely messages but was it practical to try to live by them? It certainly hadn't simplified things. Now in addition to all the fears about not knowing what to do with my life, I was worried about what having this experience meant and what I was supposed to be doing with it. Would I live up to what was being asked of me? What would others say if I told them I was listening to This Voice? Wasn't this why women were burned as witches in the past?

On the plane back home to Los Angeles a few days later, I flipped through my journal remembering the passage about fear now at the beginning of this chapter and I read it again. I started writing about fear. "Fear is not the enemy. We have nothing to fear but fear itself. Fear God. Fear is an illusion and only love is real. Be Careful. Don't talk to strangers. Don't walk by yourself at night. Listen to your fears; they are a gift. The question is not whether you have fear or not but how you move through the fear. You must do the very thing you fear. FEAR is False Evidence Appearing Real." I scribbled these fragments of quotes I'd heard and things that had been repeated to me. None of them helped. My experiences with fear are much more complex than can be dealt with by a simple slogan.

I've jumped out of an airplane. I've traveled alone to foreign countries. I've left a safe full-time job as a manager in a law office to work part-time so that I could pursue an acting career. I later started my own business as a hypnotherapist and coach. I'm comfortable speaking in front of a room full of people. A large portion of my hypnotherapy practice has been devoted to helping people overcome their fears and phobias—flying, public speaking, medical procedures, dogs, spiders, job-related anxiety, agoraphobia, to name a few. I've helped hundreds of people shift their relationship to these fears using reframing, desensitization and relaxation techniques. And yet, I'm still grappling with how to work with my own fears.

Don't we have an interesting relationship with fear? Some of us court fear, loving the thrill of the roller coaster or the scary movie. Other times, fear of simple things with little physical risk can paralyze us.

Spiritual books and teachers tell us that fear is an illusion and only love is real. In the grand scheme of being an eternal spirit this is probably true. But my human self has some issues with this characterization. I find it completely unrealistic and unhelpful. Do we tell that little girl hanging on the monkey bars that her fear is an illusion? She doesn't need a spiritual lesson at that moment, she needs help! When a mother sees her child about to run into the street, she gets an adrenaline rush as she sprints for the little one who was moments ago by her side. Her love for her child and fear of what life would be like if the unthinkable happened propels her to act perhaps even without regard for her own safety. There'd be no telling that mother whose adrenaline was still pounding from the close call that her fear wasn't real.

I think most of us have stories when we listened to the messages of fear and it wasn't an illusion but a friend that helped protect us from real danger. I can think of simple examples like the time I was about to use an ATM on a very busy street next to the entrance to a shopping mall. It was the middle of the day, lots of people were around and yet the hairs on the back of my neck stood up. I turned around and there was a man in a large jacket and a ski cap on his head, even though the day was warm. He was standing so close behind me that I could almost feel his breath on my neck. Every instinct said, "Do something," as my heart began to pound. Remembering self-defense training I had taken years before, I put my hands up in a ready stance preparing to fight if necessary and issued a direct order, "You are too close—back up now!" He backed up a few feet but at the same time, hurled the word "bitch" at me. He was testing me to see if I would back down. "I might very well be a bitch but you still are too close. Back up!" I ordered. He backed up a few more steps.

I turned slightly, cancelled my transaction, took my card and walked toward a crowd of people coming out of the shopping mall nearby. I looked back at the man who hadn't moved up to the machine to use it and watched as a petite Asian woman stepped up to the ATM. She was not paying attention to her surroundings and the man was sneaking up behind her. I called out before she could put her card in the machine, "That machine isn't giving cash. There's another inside the mall." As she turned away from the machine, the man called out a litany of crude words. The woman moved quickly to my side. We went inside the mall, found a security guard, and watched from the mall door as the guard went outside and the man ran away. When I listened to that feeling's message it was fear saying, "This is trouble—pay attention!" That message was not to be discounted. It was the animal within acknowledging a threat to my immediate physical safety. Fears such as this are designed to keep us alive. They are neither illusions nor enemies, they are gifts.

Then there are those other fears, the ones that are bringing messages like, "You are not strong enough to face this challenge. You'll fail! And you'll die!" that aren't helpful, or true. Am I the only one who has fearful chatter in her head over things like making an uncomfortable phone call?

Like the monsters under the bed or in the closet of my childhood bedroom, I know that the negative chatter isn't real, but no matter how much I tell myself that, another deeper part wants to insist, "You don't understand. They are real! What if I fail? What if I can't pay my bills? What if I end up like that homeless woman from college? What if . . . . ?" I can see that these fears are more fantasy than fact but my emotional self, just like the child afraid of monsters under the bed, doesn't understand logic.

I have spent so much time thinking that my inability to defeat these fears was a failure on my part. I judged myself for not being strong enough. I wanted to get to a place where I'd never feel fear again. I wanted to prove how spiritual and loving I was. But instead, I'd often find myself much like that little girl on the monkey bars stuck and afraid to move.

We can say we want to be fearless but if we are experiencing fear, calling it the enemy only gives the fear more power. We end up stuck in fear and then stuck in the quicksand of the judgment of our fears. Could it be that admitting we need help is the very thing that frees us? Perhaps it is that call for help that opens the door to the assistance of friends, family, helpful strangers and this mysterious thing we call spirit. This rings true and sends shivers down my spine.

I take a deep breath and say this prayer: "Hello? God, angels, whoever/whatever is out there, today I am stuck in my fears. Help me move through them. Help me to discern the messages of fear and know when they are gifts to protect my physical form and when they are trickery and illusions holding me back from living. Help me to move through the fear into the something greater that is calling me."

> **When has fear been helpful to you? Where do you get stuck? What are you afraid of right now? How do you judge yourself for being afraid? Are you willing to admit the ways you need help moving through your fears? Are you willing to ask spirit and other people for that help?**

CHAPTER 2

IT'S OKAY TO BE HUMAN

You are the place where heaven and earth meet — an infinite spirit in a body that has limits. Laugh at the complexities and contradictions with a loving heart. Remember you are divine and fragile at the same time. What good is it to hate your humanness?

Let go of the need to prove or judge yourself, and instead, experience yourself. Embrace life. Make mistakes. Forgive yourself. Learn the lessons. Where is it that you feel not good enough? Where do you feel that you need to hide or keep a part of yourself a secret? Those are your opportunities to live. Be yourself without masks or drama or affect. Be who you are most embarrassed to be. When you let go of the need to be anyone but yourself, you are truly free. Your humanness is not something to be embarrassed about. You are okay — broken and vulnerable as you feel; that brokenness is part of the journey.

Love yourself, love others — with the faults you perceive and the light that is within that you may not yet be aware of. I know how powerful that spirit within you is and how beautiful it is that you chose to take this human journey. You haven't even begun to realize how wonderful and capable and special you are but neither has your neighbor. Do you think you are alone in that desire to hide? The human journey is one of discovery. It is in your most human moments seen with the eyes of spirit that you discover the beauty of life.

~~~

"Supposing you have tried and failed again and again. You may have a fresh start any moment you choose, for this thing we call "failure" is not the falling down, but the staying down."

— Mary Pickford

~~~

There is a beautiful quote by Pierre Teilhard de Chardin that often gets repeated in spiritual circles, "We are not human beings having a spiritual experience. We are spiritual beings having a human experience."[1] Yet many people I know use that saying to by-pass the human part of the experience and go straight to some sort of spiritual cliché. "It is all divine!" they say while avoiding having any real interaction with people around them. It is like they want to eliminate every part of the human experience and just live as spirit. Tell them you are struggling with something and rather than be empathetic or give you a hug, they'll cut

---

[1] Pierre Teilhard de Chardin, *The Phenomenon of Man,* English Translation by Bernard Wall and Introduction by Julian Huxley, ©1959 William Collins Sons & Co. Ltd., London and Harper & Row, Publishers Incorporated, New York.

straight to spiritual talk and try to help you see the big picture or lesson. I've been guilty of being the spiritual lesson lady myself. I suspect we do this because we are uncomfortable with our own humanness. I know how difficult it has been for me to make peace with mine.

There is a part of me that has always felt, "I must get it right." I don't know whether that comes from a past life where I really screwed something up, or having parents that expected me to do my best, or my 16 years of Catholic school education where it seemed like the most important thing I was taught was to fall into line and follow the rules— probably all of the above. Most of my life I have strived to be perfect. This standard I set for myself has generated much fear. I was always on the precipice of being discovered as I wasn't even close to perfect. I was a messy pile of contradictions that even I didn't understand.

I learned a big lesson about being human from my dog. When I brought Sadie home from the shelter, she was a broken, scared pup that was about a year old. She was a mid-sized mixed breed weighing about 25 pounds. Tan fluffy coat that curls like a cocker spaniel at her chest and long golden red hair on her body, poufs of fur at her feet and a fan-like tail that speaks more of a golden retriever than the German Shepherd mix the shelter claimed her to be. I can see the German Shepherd in her need to patrol the perimeter and the way her ears turn to tune into what is going on around her. Her name was Tequila (a name that I knew immediately would have to go) and she had been turned in by her owners, who for whatever reason decided they didn't want her anymore.

When I brought her home, everything terrified her — the coffee grinder, the vacuum and new people, especially men. She cowered and submissively peed if you reached down too suddenly to pet her. I couldn't raise my voice when she made a mistake, because even a harsh tone made her cower and leak on the carpet. I knew I needed to give her lots of positive reinforcement and love as I taught her the rules of my house so that she could trust me and other humans again.

Now over ten years later, that life is far behind her. Sadie's nickname is now Princess and she wears the title well. If the number of toys in her toy box is any indication, my friends have gotten the word that she is to be honored with gifts. She scolds me when I've been away from home too long by whining and howling as though she's got a whole story to tell me. Her favorite part of the day is her walks. At the first sign of any squirrel, she is frozen with one paw up. Once she's locked on, it is hard to get her moving until the squirrel disappears through the overhead canopy of trees. If I needed to eat squirrel, she'd be very helpful. I often get weird looks from people as I talk to Sadie on our walks. But I know she understands what I am telling her. She's a great companion. If you are a "dog" person, you probably understand this bond that I have with my "fur person" as I often call her.

One night I woke up to a noise that I couldn't immediately identify. I turned on the lights and Sadie was lying on my bed, gnawing at her foot. Her front paws were covered in mud up to her elbows. I looked at my tan comforter and white sheets covered in muddy paw prints, as well as a trail on the carpet from the doggy door to the bedroom. As I picked her up and put her in the bathtub, I noticed that it was 4 a.m. I pulled the handheld showerhead down and began to rinse the mud away. She gave me a sorrowful look that said, "What? What did I do wrong?" I looked at those sad brown eyes and said out loud — "Digging in the dirt, is what dogs do, isn't it? You were just being a dog. I'm the one that forgot to close the doggie door!" I had to soap and re-rinse several times to get her legs clean.

After toweling her off, I loaded up the washing machine. I laughed to myself, "I forgot she was a dog!" And I stopped, struck by another question: How often do I forget I am a human? Thomas Merton said, "It is true that we make many mistakes. But the biggest of them all is to be surprised at them, as if we had some hope of never making any."[2] If we are here to have a human experience, why are we so resistant and judgmental when we are doing what human beings do? Human beings make mistakes. And I've made plenty.

In 2004, I pulled my head out of the sand where it had been firmly buried in the land of denial and added up all my credit cards. I was $100,000 in debt making $50,000 a year. The story of how I got there was a mix of addictive spending, keeping up with the Jones, taking risks that didn't pan out and life catching up with my unconsciousness.

I had stepped down from a law firm management job to pursue my heart's goal of being an actress in 1993. While I still had a good job with benefits, I took a $10,000 a year pay cut and there were lots of expenses. Being part of "the business" in Los Angeles required that I look the part, and I

---

[2] Thomas Merton, *No Man is An Island*, ©1955 The Abbey of Our Lady of Gethsemani, renewed 1983 trustees of the Merton Legacy Trust, Shambhala Publications 2005, page 134.

translated that into permission to shop. Shopping had been my drug even before I started acting. Some people use alcohol or drugs to cope with their negative emotions, I turned to Nordstrom, saying, "I need something" or "I'm worth it." "I'm bored" was as good a reason as any to head to the mall, charge a nice dinner out or a vacation. But nothing I ever bought could fill the hole of "I'm not good enough" I was trying to fill. No one knew what the formula was for success in acting but everyone wanted to offer me one — lose weight, change your hair color, update your headshots or take another workshop. I was certain that I was just one more audition away from the "big payday." If you search for my acting work on the Internet you'll come up empty. No big roles on the silver screen; just a handful of reality re-enactment and infomercial roles. The experience was a fulfilling personal journey but it never paid off financially. I was one of those people who came to Hollywood, chased a dream and moved on. I don't regret it for a moment, but there was a price that was there on my credit card statements.

In early 2002 in the wake of 9/11, I switched my focus to studying hypnosis. I funded that education with a student loan and started up the business on credit. In June 2002, my mother had a stroke and I had to travel back to Illinois several times that year to help close Mom's house and move her into the assisted living home. I was in school, starting a business and only working part time at a law firm. No paid time off, limited income and lots of expenses. It was all perfect to tip me over the edge. When I started having problems paying on time and the interest rates topped over 39%, the debt started to increase exponentially. In a short time it escalated from \$50,000 to \$100,000 from interest and penalties.

I lay awake at night trying to figure a way out. I was supposed to be smarter than this. I wanted it all to go away but it wouldn't. I was in such pain and despair that, while I never actually contemplated suicide, I understood the dark hopelessness of people who saw life as so bleak and painful that they chose that option. I was in a deep pit of self-blame and loathing. I'm not proud to say it but rather than being pro-active, I hid and let my answering machine take the calls from the creditors.

Life will send you angels when you need them most. One of mine was Chellie Campbell—author of *The Wealthy Spirit*.[3] I met Chellie at a business networking event. Red hair, wearing her signature gold tennis shoes, she was a former actor who sang her introductions at the networking events, and promoted her Financial Stress Reduction Workshop™. If anyone was under financial stress it was me. I didn't have the money to pay for her workshop. I was playing a shell game of making payments, robbing one account to pay for another. I told Chellie that I needed her class but couldn't afford it and she said, "Let's get you in the class. Pay me when you can." I worked through the budgeting portion of the class and saw how the numbers just didn't add up no matter where I tried to cut back. Chellie encouraged me to file bankruptcy. "Honey, it could take you 30 years to pay off that debt and then you'd be 70 and have no savings. A responsible person knows when she has made

---

[3] Chellie Campbell, *The Wealthy Spirit, Daily Affirmations for Financial Stress Reduction*, ©2002 Chellie Campbell, Sourcebooks, Inc, Naperville, IL.

a mistake and admits it. She doesn't keep compounding that mistake." I resisted and prayed that something magical would happen to fix the situation like winning the lottery or the Publishers Clearinghouse Sweepstakes™. There weren't enough extra hours at the law firm. The business wasn't growing fast enough. I had no money to market my business. The creditors' calls continued. There was no miracle on the horizon.

Filing bankruptcy would be admitting failure and I was certain that failure would destroy me. After many sleepless nights and getting other financial counseling that encouraged me to file, I contacted an attorney. I felt vulnerable and naked, but also more real than I had in a long time. I wasn't pretending that I didn't have issues — they were all out on the table for everyone else to see. It was freeing to no longer have a dirty secret.

I know some people judged me, but not as harshly as I had judged myself. I prided myself on being a responsible person and here I was facing the ramifications of being totally irresponsible. When I admitted to friends that I could no longer afford expensive dinners out, and even going to a movie was a stretch for my budget, a few acquaintances dropped off my social calendar. Some of my friends were relieved. They couldn't afford the lifestyle we had been living together either. And many shared with me that they, too, were deeply in debt and had been pretending that everything was okay when it wasn't.

Even though my financial bottom line was zero, and my ego had taken a huge beating, my family and friends reminded me there was a "me" that was bigger than all of those things. "You have a huge heart. You are smart. You will find your way. I love you for who you are not what you have," they'd tell me when I needed it the most. They held the light for me when I was stuck in the muck. Filing bankruptcy taught me that no amount of buying things would ever help me fill that hole of "not good enough" in my heart, and at the same time opened the door for me to see there was a "me" that was still there after admitting a mistake that I thought would crush me.

A couple years later, I pumped myself up as I drove to a business networking event, putting on a happy successful face I didn't feel. I was just getting over the flu, which had caused me to cancel a full week of clients. I didn't have the cash reserves to not feel the pinch of a week without income. When I got there, I joined the group of 10 around the luncheon table. We joked as we ate. The conversation was pretty superficial until one member of the group, "Sharon," spoke in a very open vulnerable way about family challenges she was having. When it was my time to talk, Sharon inspired me. I spoke honestly about my money fears. My friend Kristi said, "Why didn't you call us? We could get a bunch of people together for a hypnosis party. Maybe we could do a past-life regression group. It would be fun!"

It would have never occurred to me to call a friend and say "hey I need some cash—any ideas for me?" That was against every script running in my head. It was needy. I was supposed to be strong. They weren't supposed to know. I was supposed to be faking it until I made it. In other words, I wasn't supposed to be human.

That day, all sorts of stories that had been hidden for years came forth. "I thought I was the only one that felt that way!" "I thought I had to hide this from everyone!" was repeated again and again. True relationship is a place where our vulnerabilities meet and are honored. We have to risk sharing the parts of ourselves that we have labeled "not okay."

So many of us judge those moments when we feel broken, uncertain or clueless. We beat ourselves with big sticks of blame, for our very human experience rather than accepting those moments as part of the journey, honoring them and learning from them. When we look at life with the eyes of spirit and love, we know our humanness is okay; in fact it's a gift and the very reason we are here. It feels good to put down the burden of perfection that we can never achieve. We signed up for this human experience. Perhaps we need to remember to say, "I'm sorry. For a moment there I forgot you were human! It's all right. You are just doing what humans do as they experience life."

> **How do you judge yourself for being human? What do you hide from others? Where in your life do you set standards for yourself that you wouldn't set for others? Can you embrace both your spirit and your humanness?**

CHAPTER 3

LETTING GO OF A GOD NAMED ART

The Divine is in the experience, the mystery, the moment of beauty that takes your breath away, the love you feel for someone that fills you with warmth, compassion for a stranger, the song that moves you to tears; and yes, in the Voice whispering to you deep inside your heart. Step into my stream of unfolding awareness.

I am love. I am creative joy. I am in all the rhythms of life that surround you. I am within you. I am in the poetry and art that inspires you. I am mysterious only because you try to understand with your mind instead of experiencing me with your heart. Find me within you. Express me in the world. Be my healing force.

No creed should take precedence over love. See the universal truths of love and compassion that are woven in your religions and myths and let go of what man has added out of fear and the desire to keep you separate from each other. Don't let the wounds of your past keep you from a relationship with the sacred within you and in the world. The most beautiful expression of spirit is living in joy and connection with all life — honoring the journey with love. It's that simple and, yes, for many that difficult.

~~~

"I do not feel obliged to believe that the same God who has endowed us with sense, reason, and intellect has intended us to forgo their use."

— Galileo Galilei

~~~

I grew up with a God named Art who was a big guy in the sky — sort of like an unpredictable Santa Claus keeping a list of who was naughty and nice. This image of God was a "dysfunctional parent." He loved you but when He got mad, look out, anything could happen — lightning bolts, floods, sending you to hell. The name Art came from a misinterpretation of the Lord's Prayer. When I was two or three years old, I heard "Our Father who is Art in Heaven." Just like I knew that people called my daddy Russ or Woody, Art was one of the names of God.

My adult life has been about learning to let go of that God named Art who never made sense to me and the religions that insisted that I believe in Him and instead finding a personal connection to the essence of the Divine. I've never been a person who could believe that one church had the True God and everyone else was screwed. It didn't make sense to me that the all powerful, all present force that many call God would say, "Until some missionaries of a specific church come to your land and you learn to call me by the name those people use, until you read that book and go to that Church right there — that one and only that one, I won't let you know me!"

I think of the different religions as though they are jazz ensembles. Each one is taking an experience of the Divine, capturing the theme and interpreting it. Sometimes there is beautiful music and that song helps people find the best in themselves. Sometimes the song becomes discordant—more about the very human qualities of ego, politics and fear rather than a connection to the Divine Source of Life. So many people believe that their religion was handed to them directly by God and that their Holy Books present the only way. I feel more comfortable when I think of all the versions of God in different religions as archetypes or metaphors that describe God but aren't actually God. They are representations of the indescribable; much like a photograph or a painting of the Grand Canyon can't possibly capture the grandeur of being there. Religions do their best to capture someone's experience of the Divine but they also throw in a lot of human stuff echoing tribal notions of how we are separate and different from each other. I cannot believe in a Divine spirit that would want us to be less loving and divide ourselves into the "in" group and the "out" group.

I needed to make peace with my religious upbringing, and the personal and societal wounds I saw done in the name of God before I could accept this experience of The Voice. Because as much as I didn't want to call The Voice God, I knew I was having an intensely spiritual experience. I felt a connection with the Divine in these moments that was definitely out of sync with what I grew up believing was possible for me.

I grew up in a devoutly Catholic home. My parents weren't just Christmas/Easter Catholics, as they called those people who only made it to Church on the major holidays.

They went to church every Sunday and were actively involved in the parish. I loved my parents and knew their beliefs fit them like a glove, but for me many of those beliefs were more like a pair of shoes that pinched and rubbed in the wrong places. The pinch started pretty early.

I was eight and outraged. Boys in my class were learning to serve as altar boys. Why were there no girl altar servers? This has changed in the intervening years, but when I was growing up I was told, "No. You can't do it because you are a girl." The job didn't seem to require a boy — after all I could light candles and pour little cruets with water and wine into a cup for the priest. It was bigger than being an altar server. I didn't see any reason why women couldn't do what the priests were doing either. It made steam come out of my young pre-adolescent ears. Growing up in the 1960s and 70s, the feminist movement was telling me I could do anything, be anyone when I grew up, except in my church where women were second-class citizens. My journey away from traditional religions probably began that day but took many more years to be complete.

When I was nine, the nuns would have us line up to go to confession. Standing in the long aisle of the church next to the blonde wood pews in my navy blue jumper, crisp white uniform blouse, saddle shoes and knee socks, I'd shift back and forth, closing my eyes as I waited in line as I would see the adults do when they went to confession. Then I'd panic as I tried to come up with what I was going to say. Opening my eyes, I'd stare at the Stations of the Cross plaques on the walls between the golden textured glass windows around the outside the perimeter of the church. Jesus died for my sins and yet I couldn't think of anything I had done wrong.

What was I going to confess? Why was I blank? The nuns insisted we were sinners and always had things to confess. If Jesus died for me, I'd better have a list of rules that I had broken so they could be wiped away like a chalkboard being erased. Confession caused me immense stress until I figured out my strategy. I'd make up some sins and end with the sin, "I lied." I'd get absolution for sins I didn't do and for the lie I did tell. I can laugh now. I'm pretty sure this is not what the nuns intended.

Ironically, it was the excellent education that I received in Catholic schools that led to my deepest questioning. How did a religion which started with "love God, love yourself and love your neighbor, pray for your enemies and let the person without sin caste the first stone" become all about rules and "I'm unworthy because I'm a sinner?" If God is The Ultimate, The All Knowing, you'd think "He'd" be pretty secure with Himself. What could God be jealous of? People who are secure in how awesome they are don't need to be jealous, do they? Why would God be any different? And why was God always portrayed as a He? If God is everywhere and in everything, where was the feminine face of God? Was God really hung up on dietary rules, sexual rules, and rules about who can marry?

In all my questioning I never doubted that there was an invisible thread that connects us all; a beautiful and loving creative force that reveals itself to us in the whispers of our hearts and in the experiences of the amazing miracles and mysteries of the world. This spirit connection is everywhere. A baby smiles, my heart melts. Spirit is there. My dog is so happy that I am home that she runs around the house unable to contain her joy. The Divine is there. A dear friend shares her deepest fears and vulnerabilities and our hearts connect. The sacred is there. I am overawed by the grandeur of the mountains capped with snow and the field of flowers alongside the road. Absolute Beauty is there. The whispers pour onto the page. I am certain there is something sacred there. My heart breaks open because a loved one dies; and yes, even in that moment, there is beauty and holiness. In tragedy and disasters there are those moments we see God — not as a wrathful being wreaking havoc but in the beauty of the love as people reach out to help each other. And maybe even in those tragedies, maybe there is a Divine plan as my mother would say. But I see it more in the cosmic sense of an orderly universe than in a man named Art in heaven with a master playbook.

There is a Source like a sacred spring from which all flows. That mystery is where I came from and where I sense I'll be returning to when my time in this body is done. My heart feels it is true. I'm more interested in experiencing that Divine mystery than trying to find one religious expression with a set of rules to follow. The idea of a Divine force that rules by intimidation and wants me to be afraid of It, seems so out of alignment with a loving force that I have to let it go.

For the last thirty years I have been exploring different religions and philosophies. I've been nurtured by Buddhist and Hindu teachings. I liked the less judgmental attitude and inclusiveness found in many of the New Thought churches. I return to some of the teachings of my childhood, and hear them with new ears. "Love your neighbor. Be compassionate. Don't judge. Seek and ye shall find. Ask and it is given. Listen and you shall hear." Those last ones sound like what happened when I called out, "What do you want me to do?" from a place deep inside of true surrender and The Voice answered. There is a reason why those teachings have withstood the test of time. They are universal truths.

I can gather the wisdom and let go of those experiences, beliefs and rules that used to block me—including that cranky old God named Art. Making this shift allows me to let go of the fear embedded in those traditions and to embrace a Divine force that is always present and active in my life. I'm not trying to find or create a new religion or a new set of rules. The codified belief structures can get in the way of connection with that Source and others. Arguing what I believe about God with others and trying to prove I'm right will get me nowhere. Instead, I commit to the moment-to-moment experience of the Sacred Mystery that is life itself and how that wonderful Divine presence reveals itself to me and in the world. Living the Sacred Mystery is so much more powerful than believing in a set of rules or a God named Art.

> **What was your experience of spirituality and faith growing up? Did your experience nurture you? Do you feel injured by your religious upbringing or by religion in general? Have you had to sift for gold? Or have you thrown it all away? Are there any spiritual injuries or beliefs you need to look at before you can fully embrace living connected to the highest Voice within you?**

CHAPTER 4

EMBRACING THE WOO-WOO

Trust the authentic voice deep inside you. This quiet voice of Loving Truth will not lead you anywhere but to a fuller expression of you. Listen. Embrace it and make it your life's mission to know it more and more intimately each passing day.

You keep looking for the logic in what is happening. This is not a brain exercise; it is a heart experience. Embrace the sacred in you. It is your choice to put your faith in science, in religion, in money, in work, in others or in the connection with this presence that calls to your soul. Embrace the unseen, the unspoken, the things known about — not of the mind but of the heart. Step into the stream of unfolding awareness. Listen. Your authentic self is one with the universe. Let your spirit join your humanness in this beautiful dance called life. Share what you hear, your power, your talents and gifts for the good of all. Tune in. Connect now and live the Mystery.

~~~
**"Intuition, not intellect, is the 'open sesame' of yourself." — Albert Einstein**
~~~

I have now joined the ranks of those people in Los Angeles who speak in New Age code. "The Voice Within is sharing messages with me." How far is that from those people who walk around saying, "My guides are telling me I shouldn't go to that movie" or "I see your aura and it's beautiful"? I have lived in California for over 20 years so I'm used to being around *woo-woo* people who steep themselves in the New Age or ancient wisdom, and claim to be mystics, psychics or channels of ancient spirits. I have maintained a healthy skepticism when people claim some grand connection to the spirit world. It's not that I didn't believe it was possible, maybe for them, but I never considered that I would be one of the people making these claims.

Was I really supposed to throw out everything logical I knew and just trust some voice that was telling me vague things like *embrace the unseen*? I wanted a map or clear-cut directions of how you move from being scared to sacred. Instead, I got the message *"Trust the authentic voice deep inside you."* Trust it? Part of me wanted to put my fingers in my ears and chant like a child, "LALALALA I can't hear you!" I could block it temporarily by distracting myself, but it kept coming back like an ear worm—that song that gets stuck in your head and no matter how hard you try you keep hearing it.

What was I supposed to do with this information? It wasn't like it was given to me in any publishable form. And even as I wrote that question down, I heard, *"Oh ye of little faith!"* and thought it funny that that Bible verse would pop into my head. Writing an hour a day taking down the notes and then creating something from them wasn't exactly like being asked to walk on water, was it? Then I heard the song in my head that I learned as a child based on the lilies of the field passage from Matthew 6:25–34 telling me not to worry about what to wear or what to eat but to leave everything in God's hands. I hadn't thought of that song in 30 years or more. Maybe my spirit or subconscious was using that song to communicate with me.

I decided to treat it like an experiment. I'd do what I committed to — write an hour a day — and see how it worked and where it led me. If the experiment went bad, I would stop. I would often find myself in bed, exhausted with the light off, and I'd have this nagging feeling that wouldn't let me settle down. Then I'd realize that I hadn't written that day. I'd have to get out of bed and write or I couldn't sleep. Several nights I tried to ignore the urging. "I'm tired. I'll write tomorrow!" I'd toss and turn until I had to get out of bed. "Okay you win! I'll write. Are you happy now?"

I also wasn't prepared for the number of times The Voice would pop into my head while driving, showering or walking the dog. I ended up with notes scribbled on stray pieces of paper, on my hand, voice notes on my cell phone all trying to capture the messages that were coming to me. It was as though I had turned on a faucet and couldn't turn it off.

"Just be with what is happening right now; don't try to figure it all out. Enjoy the beauty of the experience today," The Voice told me. I had never been particularly good about staying in the moment and not worrying about what comes next, but in this case I really didn't have much choice. There was no way

to know where this experience was leading. But I did know that when I showed up at that journal, the experience was powerful.

As I wrote, I remembered other experiences that I had written off or forgotten where The Voice had spoken to me in the past. In my hypnotherapy practice, there were times that clients would tell me their problems and I would have no idea what direction to take as I led them into hypnosis through the relaxation. My stomach would do a small flip as I would scramble for what to say or what exercise to use to help them. I'd say a silent prayer, "Help me!" and take a deep breath and hope that I'd be inspired. After the session was over the client would say, "That thing you said was amazing! Could you repeat that so I could write it down?" Sometimes I'd have a vague memory of marveling at the words that were coming out of my mouth as I said them but after the fact, I couldn't recall anything specific about what I said. It was as though I channeled the whole session from the moment I said, "Help!"

I had one client who was struggling with an issue at work.[4] A thought inside my head said to me, "Ask her about her brother." I resisted because I didn't even know whether she had a brother. She had never mentioned a brother in the many sessions we had spent together; and what could her brother have to do with this work issue anyway? "Ask her about her brother." I ignored The Voice again. But the impulse persisted like a fly buzzing around in my head that I couldn't get rid of: "Ask her about her brother." So after the third (or possibly the twelfth) time, I tried to figure out how I

---

[4] I've omitted or changed identifying circumstances in my clients' stories to protect their privacy.

was going to ask about a brother I didn't even know she had. Finally I said, "I don't know whether this means anything but I keep getting an impulse to ask about your brother. Does anything about a brother or sibling relate to this issue?" She looked at me incredulously and said, "This is exactly what used to happen with my brother. I haven't spoken with him for more than 20 years." She had never connected the issue she was having with a resentment she still had for her brother. As she explained, I understood there were valid reasons for cutting her brother out of her life but something about that old relationship was playing out in her relationships in the work place. We worked on releasing the anger and shifting her perception of herself. A few weeks later she reported that the issue at work resolved itself without her having to confront her co-workers.

If I had been raised in a different culture or family I might have a better understanding of connecting to that intuitive voice or channeling information from some sort of higher consciousness. There are families where psychic skills are just one of the family traits. Not mine.

My mother, Lucille, was born into a Bohemian Catholic family in Prairie du Chien, Wisconsin. When I say Bohemian I don't mean artsy, gypsy fortune tellers. My great-grandparents came to the United States from the area of the Czech Republic that was once the country of Bohemia. Mom's side of the family was filled with steadfast, hard-working people who were stoic about the hardships they faced but quick with a laugh and very devoted to their faith. My father, Russell, was born near Sparta, Wisconsin and called himself a "Heinz 57," meaning a mix of ethnicities but primarily English, German and Irish. He was raised

Methodist but converted to the Catholic faith to marry my mom.

They were practical people who created good lives on a working-class income. Dad was a linotype press operator for the local newspaper. Mom was a stay-at-home mom until I was in second grade and then a bookkeeper for an accountant. Dad was 46; Mom was 38 when I was born. I have one sister, Luanne, who is eight years older than me. I was a surprise baby. My parents had tried for years to have a second child and had resigned themselves that it wasn't to be and then, "Surprise!" I never felt unwanted. In fact, if anything I felt cherished — especially by my Dad with whom I had a special bond.

I grew up in Rockford, Illinois, a machine-tool manufacturing town known at one time (to its inhabitants' chagrin) as the "Screw Capital of the World" because of the billions of screws, bolts and fasteners its factories produced. Rockford is about twenty miles from the Illinois-Wisconsin border with a metropolitan population of around 150,000. Although it was a good-sized city by most people's standards, it had small-town values. Everyone I knew went to church, knew their neighbors and rooted for their favorite high school football team. The only reference point I had for people who heard spirit voices were the *woo-woo* types, the crazy types like that homeless lady from college and the stories of the mystics and saints from the Catholic Church. I wasn't looking to be canonized anytime soon. My list of reasons why I couldn't be a saint was long. I knew I wasn't crazy. That left *woo-woo*.

I could say I was imagining things. I could say that I was smart and much of this was just good common sense. But none of what my logical mind tried to tell me could take away the love and energy I felt when there was that shift and The Voice took over. The experience had more power than anything I could come up with in my mind to explain it away. I searched for other experiences that weren't logical but that I was comfortable with. Following your heart is often in direct conflict with what some would say is logical or practical. I knew that the unseen, unspoken power of love was real. I also knew that we could love someone and be totally upset by something they had done. Maybe I needed to be able to hold the opposing viewpoints on this experience: "This doesn't seem logical, and it seems real. It seems powerful, magical and ridiculous at the same time and it seems like the most important thing I can do right now."

I continued to listen and write down the messages. Each time I did, it felt more and more like coming home — a home I had forgotten I even had. The Voice was the most direct real spiritual experience I had ever had in my life. When I heard it, I was filled with love and peace. So what was my choice? I could spend my energy trying to block the experience or follow the *woo-woo*. I opted to continue to embrace the *woo-woo* and see where it took me.

> **What judgments do you have about connecting directly with spirit, using your intuition, or getting messages from the beyond? Are there times when your heart or spirit tells you one thing and your mind tells you something else? Are you willing to embrace the contradictions? Are you willing to embrace what many call *woo-woo*?**

CHAPTER 5

GET OUT OF YOUR COMFORT ZONE
AND PLAY

Say yes to the adventure of life. Deepen your connection to Joy
— the energy that reminds you who you are. Savor the joy in doing
whether by the world's standard it is labeled ugly or not good
enough. Think of the things you have given up that you loved
because you judged them. Did you stop playing baseball because
you'd never be a pro? Did you stop singing because you judged
your voice? Did you stop loving because you might get hurt?

You choose to live and expand, or shut down. You can fill
yourself with things that support and nurture you or pretend that
it is too dangerous and hide away from who you really are. Know
that death isn't the worst thing — dying without ever fully living is.

In resisting your capacity for joy now in search of some far-off
idea of perfection, you live in the idea of "what is supposed to be"
and ignore the beauty that is now. Stop trying so hard to get it
right and enjoy the ride. Laugh, sing, dance and play. Participate

with gusto — even if you think you might snort, sing off key, have two left feet or make a fool of yourself. Have fun! Commit to being the music of life instead of turning off the player and shutting yourself away.

Get out of your comfort zone and play. Try and see what works and what doesn't. Find your own way. What would your spirit and soul call you to do today? Do something — small or big. Do what gives you true joy — that makes your spirit say "this is living." Do that which scares you. Do that which expands your capacity to love. Do it well or poorly. Don't wait. Live! Begin now!

~~~

"Life is rarely as serious as we believe it to be, and when we recognize this fact, it responds by giving us more and more opportunities to play."
— Osho/Deva Padma

~~~

You might think that I'd say that the most important thing that connected me to The Voice was learning to be still enough to listen. You'd be wrong. I can trace the beginning of The Voice guiding me to something even more fundamental than stillness — play and joy.

When we were young, we experienced the whole world as an opportunity to explore and express ourselves. As adults, many of us stuff that authentic childlike, open and free part of ourselves down somewhere deep inside, and judge play as something frivolous rather than an essential expression of who we are.

When clients say their lives aren't working, I ask, "When was the last time you did something for no reason other than it makes you happy?" I often get a blank stare in return. Many of us have created lives where doing something fun is actually out of our comfort zone. We may play organized sports or have a hobby but doing something for pure joy, risking being seen as silly, isn't comfortable.

I spent many years focused on getting things done, disconnected from my joy. It took a reality television show and a rock singer from Chicago to remind me that those parts we ignore, aren't gone, just stuffed deep inside waiting for the opportunity to enrich our lives.

When I was a junior at Marquette University, I was the first woman to manage the university's radio station, WMUR. I was the squeaky clean Midwestern girl tagging along with my programming and music director to the punk and rock clubs. I'd always loved music but I didn't know much about the alternative 80s music we played on the station. I had worked my way up through the ranks of the news division. Bands like: Wall of Voodoo, The Clash, Bad Brains, Bow Wow Wow and local bands like Those Xcleavers, Yipes!, The Oil Tasters and The Tense Experts were all new to me.

I was the one who stood stunned when a girl decided to shave her head in the restroom of the Stoned Toad with a straight razor while I waited to wash my hands or when the Bad Brains started tipping tables over as they performed. I felt like a fish out of water at those clubs with the patrons, bands and DJs who were so much "hipper" than I was. I wanted to be a "wild child," but I just wasn't—I was the one who followed the rules. But it was worth any discomfort I might feel to hear the music, especially when something was edgy or different. I fantasized about working for a record company and being the one to discover the next new band, but put that part of me on the shelf and found a practical job after college working as a sales manager at Macy's. This was the beginning of years of compromise, where I told myself that the things that my heart was drawn to weren't for me because they were scary and not practical.

During the summer of 2005, I was working a part-time night job at a law firm while developing my coaching practice. As hard as I worked, I could not seem to get ahead. Fun wasn't on my list. One rare night at home, I turned on the TV. I flipped through the channels and stumbled on a reality show called *Rock Star INXS*. I watched as a tall, lean, blonde singer from Chicago, Marty Casey, stood with both hands on the microphone, one foot forward with knee bent and started to sing. I thought, "This guy has 'it'!" — that indefinable magic that captures the audience and makes them want more.

I watched the show religiously that summer and was disappointed when "my guy" Marty didn't win but delighted when INXS asked Marty and his band, Lovehammers, to open for their upcoming tour.

Months later, I thought to myself, "INXS and Lovehammers are coming to Los Angeles and you didn't buy a ticket." The show was sold out but I decided to check eBay. A tenth row single ticket called my name. Pairs of tickets were expensive but I had a good chance of getting that single ticket as the closing time on the auction was only a few hours away and I would be the first bidder. As I contemplated going to a concert alone, fear kicked up but The Voice inside insistently said, *"Bid on the ticket."* I put in my bid and went to bed. The next morning, I got the notification that I had won with my opening bid of $12 less than the face value of the ticket. Several days later, Lovehammers announced a midnight show at the Viper Room on Sunset Strip after the INXS concert. Was I really thinking about going to two shows by myself in one night? Wasn't that a little obsessive? The Voice again said, *"Buy the ticket."* I thought for only a moment and then did just that, amazed at how far out of my comfort zone I was and how giddy I was at the same time.

The evening of the show came. I panicked. Each time I heard a voice in my head say, "You can stay home," another more insistent voice would said, *"Go! You'll have fun!"* When Lovehammers took the stage, the pounding drums of their song Ultrasound, reminded me of how much I loved live music. Marty appeared and took command of the crowd with one-on-one eye contact—seducing and daring us to come along on this rock 'n' roll ride. He spun, jumped and bent over backwards as he sang. He became the "mad conductor" (a move familiar to those who watched *Rock Star*). He walked out into the audience and stood on the back of a seat with the crowd surrounding him. I looked around and realized that the band had a cynical LA crowd on their feet for an opening act. So caught up in the experience, I forgot I was alone at the concert.

Later that night at the Viper Room, I chatted with other fans as we waited in the packed room for the band to appear. And when they took the stage, the room thumped and pounded with the energy of the bass, the drums, and I felt a special connection with everyone there as we sang along, "Hold on to your head when your heart is broken. Clouds will clear and the sun will shine once again. Hold on to my hand if you feel like jumping, I will be there till the end of time."[5] I was in a room full of friends I had never met before united by the music. For the first time since my struggle with my bankruptcy, I felt free and happy. I was more alive than I had been in years.

A couple of months later, I received a phone message from Chris, one of the women who I had met at the INXS show. She asked me if I wanted to see Lovehammers in Las Vegas at the Hard Rock Hotel the next evening. They were playing a private show and one of the women she knew had gotten twelve free tickets for the show. I didn't hesitate. I said, "I'll be there," even though I was teaching a stress management class the next day at lunch time at an aerospace company in Irvine. Even though I didn't have the money for an airline ticket so I would have to drive to Vegas and then turn around the next morning and drive back in order to be back in LA by 5 p.m. on Friday to work my shift at the law firm. Driving my 1991 Chrysler five hours to Vegas to see a concert was risky. At 15 years old, it was no longer the most reliable car, but nothing was going to keep me from seeing that show.

The next day after my presentation, I changed out of my business clothes and got on the road. As I drove to Vegas, I got caught in a long construction delay. I had to run the heater to keep the car from overheating. I drank lots of water and then worried about finding a bathroom as I inched my way across the desert. I sweated and fretted about getting to Vegas on time as I waited in line with a 100 other people for a bathroom at one of the only mom & pop businesses along that stretch of road. I got back in the car and asked God or

---

[5] Hold On, ©2006 Martin Casey, Bob Kourelis, Dino Kourelis, William Sawilchik used by permission.

the concert fairy or whoever handles these lucky occurrences on the other side, "You wouldn't get me a free ticket to a show and then have me miss it because of traffic—would you?" I heard nothing but kept driving on faith. I pulled into the hotel just in time to take a quick shower to wash the sweat from the hot desert ride off my body and meet up with the group for the show. I was once again transported by the music.

After the show, the band came out and I decided since the crowd was small, I was going to try to say hello to Marty. I just wanted to thank him for inspiring me to bust out of my comfort zone. Chris said, "I'll take your picture if you take mine," as we made our way across the bar. I'm a pretty chatty person and have never had a problem talking with strangers but I walked up to Marty and I could barely speak. I looked at him and pointed at my friend with the camera— and mumbled something witty like, "Picture—would you?" He put his arm around me and we took the picture. I said "thanks" and he turned to speak to the next person. When it was my turn to take Chris's picture, I couldn't even operate her camera. The lens cap was still on and it was dark when I looked through the viewfinder. I snapped pictures of the blackness. My brain cells had officially turned to mush. What was going on? I felt like a gauche twelve-year-old and just as unsure of how to conduct myself. Who was this person? I was mortified and giddy at the same time.

We all went to another bar at the hotel to hang out. I bumped into Marty again. Thankfully, I was a little more articulate at that point, and I was able to thank him for the inspiration and say that the Viper Room show was probably one of the best shows I had ever seen. He said, "It was special, wasn't it?" We talked a few more minutes. I was a fountain of scintillating conversation, blabbering about my drive across the desert to see him and how I'd never done anything like that before in my life. A story I know he heard again and again that night. I wished I had something witty or original to say, but I had to settle for my simple "thank you." We separated so he could get a beer. I watched the people surrounding Marty and the rest of the band. Some people just like me wanting to say hello; others probably hoping for more. On some level, I had judged my behavior driving to Vegas as the actions of a middle-aged woman trying to become a groupie. The thought was a little embarrassing and scary to me. Relieved that I had no impulse to try to slip anyone a room key, I went back to my room alone and went to sleep with a smile on my face from how much I had enjoyed the evening.

The next morning at 10:30 a.m., I was out the door of the hotel and driving back to LA so I could be at my law firm job on time. It was a long trip. The previous 24 hours seemed surreal, almost like someone else had actually made the trip. I kept laughing as I thought of how crazy the whole thing was.

Over the next two years, I became a little obsessed. I saw Lovehammers perform at least ten more times. Fortunately the band is from Chicago near my family, so I could time my visits to coincide with shows. But I also planned several road trips for the sole purpose of seeing the band play. Funny, when I first typed that sentence I typed "soul purpose" instead of "sole purpose." Perhaps the first is true. These outings nourished a part of me that I had stuffed down and told myself didn't matter.

After each show, I would notice that business was improving. I was booking more presentations, which led to more private clients. I hadn't done any additional marketing or promotions. The only thing I had done differently was go to those concerts. I made great friends, who loved music like I did, among the Hammerheads, as fans of the band call themselves. In the joy that I felt reconnecting with the part of me that loves music, I remembered what fun and play felt like, and that joy radiated out and attracted new opportunities for me. I understood something that had never clicked in my reading of books on the law of attraction. It isn't just what you visualize or affirm that creates and attracts things into your life; it is the energy you live. While my Lovehammers fever has mellowed, I am so thankful to Marty, Bob, Billy and Dino for helping me reclaim that part of me that I had buried. They reminded me that life was bigger than simply getting by and through them I have made friends around the world.

Doing what we love to do is claiming our uniqueness and expressing our individual selves in the world. Young children don't judge whether their art work is perfect, whether they sing off key or dance funny. They just enjoy coloring or painting, singing and doing that funny dance.

Skipping like a child, dancing in your underwear in your living room to a great song, painting with acrylics, swinging on a swing in the park, hiking on a nature trail, playing hooky one afternoon and going to the beach, buying yourself a small bunch of flowers, getting down on the floor and playing with the dog or going to a concert may or may not be on your joy list, but they are on mine. These things remind me of who I am and why I'm here—to fully experience my life. And when I allow myself joy in the simple things, life works in magical and amazing ways.

I remember this experience each time I encourage clients to step out and play. I'm connecting them with a truth. If we don't feed our capacity for joy, often we end up living in a world that seems gray and lifeless. When we feel stuck, one of the best solutions is not to work harder but to take some time to step away, get out of our routines and go play. It might feel uncomfortable at first, but most adventures are. When we cultivate a relationship with our joy, our hearts and spirits expand and we remember who we are. You don't have to follow a rock band—just step out and do something a little out of your normal routine—that thing that makes you a little scared, a little embarrassed and at the same time makes your heart sing!

> **How attuned are you to what makes your heart sing? Have you heard a whisper "That would be fun!" or "Buy a ticket?" When can you add some joy and play to your life? No you don't have to follow a rock band—just follow what makes your heart sing!**

CHAPTER 6

THE INNER MARSHMALLOW

Have no fear of the soft sweet tender places inside. It is there you experience the richness of life – the joy of connection, the pain of loss, the fire of anger, the dull ache of wanting more, the giddiness of exploring something new, the fear of not being ready, the warmth and comfort of love, the laughter that makes your sides ache. Rejoice that you are alive. If you try to live untouched by certain feelings, you will not fully live. Choose a full color existence rather than limiting your palette. Live full out and know that will involve beautiful highs and lows.

If you feel you are being broken, let it happen and let the light in. As you experience this trauma, you ride the shooting star that illuminates your path. Dark, unwanted, ugly moments, have their purpose. Understanding comes later. Be with each passing feeling without adding to the drama.

In that tender place, you are stronger than you know. In that tender place, you are connected to everyone who has laughed and cried and fought and feared. The one, who has lost, has a special open heart for others who are grieving. Let your feelings help you know love and compassion for all who have felt the way you feel.

Honor yourself in your journey, while you honor all those around you. That soft tender place keeps you connected to the universal heart. Feel and know yourself.

~~~

"Those who don't know how to weep with their whole heart, don't know how to laugh either." — Golda Meir

~~~

My mom and dad came of age in the Depression and World War II. Their generation didn't speak about or analyze their feelings; it just wasn't done. As a child I understood that it was easier for Mom to show her love than speak it. I knew she loved me, but I still craved the words. I don't remember her actually saying the words, "I love you" during my childhood. She demonstrated her love in actions. She was an expert seamstress who would stay up late sewing clothes for my sister and me. Every stitch contained love. There wasn't a special event that mom didn't sew a beautiful gown for my sister or me, including my sister's wedding. She helped my friends with their sewing projects with patience, helping rescue projects that should have been beyond repair. When I was young she baked cookies and chauffeured my friends and me to events. She did everything that a wife and mother in the 1960s and 1970s did and she did it beautifully. That was the "good mom."

But there was the other side where something would explode inside her and she would slam cupboard doors, and yell. I would go hide in the bathroom and lock the door. I never knew what would set her off. Sometimes it was about something I did like leaving shoes around the house. Other times it was about something she did like accidentally dropping an egg on the floor.

When Mom was in a bad mood, my father would say to me, "Carol, she's a good woman. I know she can be difficult, but she's doing the best she can." It always amazed me that my dad loved her unconditionally even when she was out of control. And I thank him for that! Many times in the midst of these moments, my father would often look at me and say, "You want to go for ice cream?" We'd head out, giving Mom space to cool off. This is probably why ice cream is still my favorite comfort food. Most times when we'd come home, all was well again until the next time.

Still, these explosive moments bothered me. "When I grow up, I'm out of here. I'm moving far away!" I also promised myself when I grew up I would be like a turtle. I'd have a hard shell to protect myself and I wouldn't roll over and show anyone my soft spots. I'd protect that tender place inside. I wanted laughter, love and joy. I wanted to avoid pain, fear and sadness. I wouldn't let myself ever show anger and rage. I wouldn't be like my mother.

Once out on my own, I placed a high value on being nice and not making waves. I worked hard as my parents taught me to do. But occasionally, I'd be so angry or upset, and having no skills in how to talk about my frustration, I'd explode or end up in tears so overwhelming that I couldn't talk. I hated anger. I just had to work harder to stuff it down so it didn't win.

I overate looking for comfort in food; I maxed out my credit cards trying to fill the hole deep inside with new clothes and expensive dinners. I stuffed myself into a box trying to be what others wanted me to be. I became less and less "me." The sad thing was that I didn't even know who "me" was. I spent so much time trying to please others and following the rules that it was as though I had taped my authentic self's mouth shut with duct tape as I shoved the real me in the box. Something inside me was screaming, "Let me out. Listen to me!" I kept myself too busy to listen.

Ten years after college, I decided to take an acting class for fun. Acting was something I had always wanted to do, but didn't believe I could follow that dream because it wasn't practical. The first class hooked me. A year later, I negotiated a job change so that I would have time to pursue this passion. I got an agent on my first mailing, booked a part in the first student film I auditioned for and later worked in infomercials and a few reality re-enactment television shows. I was certain that this is what the universe wanted me to do. It was, not because I was destined to be a star but because the experiences that I had in acting were pivotal to my personal and spiritual development.

Little did I know that there is a big difference between pretending to feel and acting authentically. Acting challenged me to get back in touch with all those emotions I had judged and pushed down in my childhood. Tears came easy. They always have. I surprise people at how mushy and sentimental I am. But anger was another story.

One day in acting class in one of those basement theaters in Hollywood, I was working on a scene about a married couple on the verge of a divorce. My acting teacher stopped me and said, "He just said something awful to you in this scene. What do you feel?" Feel? I didn't feel anything. I tried to come up with the right answer. I wish I could remember the actual words that were said to me in the scene. I can't even remember anything about the actual play or TV show that the material came from. All I remember is feeling caught—I stood there blinking and searching for a feeling. I had none. I was flunking a test. I had achieved my childhood goal of becoming the turtle and tucking myself safe inside the shell and quietly saying inside, "No one is going to touch me with that anger!"

"You need access to all of your feelings to be a good actor. People won't want to pay to watch you cope. They want to watch you do what real people do—struggle with their emotions, sometimes win and sometimes lose. You are going to have to learn to be comfortable being uncomfortable. That is the only way you'll be able to do what an actor does. People don't want to watch you pretend to be devastated. They want you to *be* devastated by what someone says to you," my teacher coached me. This really wasn't what I had signed up for. I wanted to *act*. I didn't want to *feel* those messy feelings.

It sounds rather silly to admit that I thought I could act without feeling. Actors go places intentionally that most of us would rather avoid. If learning to deal with my emotions and allowing myself to feel anger were part of being a good actor, I decided I'd better dive in and get to work. I worked with therapists, took workshops and classes to be a more authentic actor. I succeeded. When I made breakthroughs and was able to be angry in a scene, I'd celebrate. There was a rush to creating a character that was authentic.

Through acting I also became a more compassionate human being. No matter how unlikeable a character's actions may appear, the actor has to understand what makes that person tick. I would look for what the story was underneath the actions. I didn't have to know what the playwright or screenwriter intended, I just had to make up a story for me that would help me understand why I would act the way the character would act. For example one time in a scene study class, I was paired with a lovely man to play a scene as husband and wife. The only problem was there was no chemistry between us. How was I going to make this painful scene about a father walking out on his wife because their child was born with Down's syndrome work? I realized the essence of the scene was about betrayal, not any form of sexual chemistry. So in my mind I told myself stories of how this was my gay best friend who had promised to co-parent with me and now because the child wasn't perfect he was walking away. The scene played beautifully and no one knew how I had tricked myself to make it work. Writing a helpful back story can work in real life too.

I used this technique to explore my relationship with my mother. Those rages had to come from somewhere. I put myself in her shoes, imagining I had lived her life. What would cause me to have those moments where I'd just snap? I saw an amazing, smart, creative woman trapped in an era where she was supposed to be the perfect 60s housewife. Wouldn't trying to live up to June Cleaver make anyone angry, especially when no one appreciated it?

The generations who grew up during the Depression and World War II had to tuck away many of their personal desires to focus on surviving. What dreams had she buried during the war? Did she ever get to reclaim those parts of herself or was she seeing something in me that she never had? Was this why I often felt that she was angry with me? I don't know whether any of my guesses were true, but the stories I made up helped me let go of my hurt and judgment. She wasn't doing anything to me — she was just doing the best she could. Just like we all do.

There were challenges in our relationship especially after my father passed away. Dad had been the buffer. Once I moved away from home Mom and I could avoid most conflicts and pretend that everything was okay. I say pretend because we didn't talk about what was bothering us. Our pattern was passive aggressive. When I stepped down from my management job to pursue acting, Mom showed her dislike or fear of my choice by asking, "How's that *little* acting thing you are doing going?" Ouch! I was living my dream, following my passion and Mom reduced it to a "little thing" with a twist of a word. I'd vacillate between yelling back, making a sarcastic comment or freezing up and then griping to someone later about how unsupportive Mom was.

It took me several years to be able to step back, take a deep breath and calmly ask, "What do you mean?" or "I'm wondering what is bothering you that you would say that," when Mom would throw out one of her quips. Mom would sputter and normally change the subject in response. After a while the barbs stopped. She might have been thinking them but she didn't say them. I realized Mom didn't have the skills to say what was bothering her. Maybe she didn't even know. I certainly didn't have the skills or courage to step forward and try to talk about it. Over time I realized that I didn't need to change her as much as I needed to shift how I saw her and labeled her behavior. If I told myself that Mom was nervous for me and didn't know how to talk about it, when she took a dig at my acting choice, I felt better—whether it was true or not.

My mom always said, "You'll appreciate me when you are older." And sometimes, she'd issue the mother's curse, "I hope you have a daughter just like you one day!" I have never fulfilled the curse as I've never had children, but Mom was right on the first one. I do appreciate her completely. She was the perfect mother for me even though I needed to work on my perceptions and stories to be able to see it. As children we see our parents as all powerful. Now as an adult I can understand that she had a soft tender place inside that she was trying to protect.

I call this soft, sweet, tender place the inner marshmallow. It is that place that can melt when warmed by love and can easily get scorched when exposed to the fire of intense feeling. We see it in children who live with their feelings in the moment out there for all of us to see. As babies and small children, we cried when we were sad or uncomfortable. We said no or shook our heads vehemently if we didn't like something, maybe even spitting back out food that we didn't like. We had meltdowns when we were overtired and couldn't sooth ourselves. That is completely normal but no one wants to live or work with an adult who throws a literal or metaphorical tantrum each time something doesn't go his way.

Our socialization tells us it is wrong to express those feelings so dramatically and many of us began to think that it was wrong to have this tender place inside. We found various ways to hide or protect it. We sorted our emotions into acceptable and unacceptable feelings. We did everything we could to escape from those unacceptable feelings—

avoiding situations where they might come up, or once they arose, pushing them away and denying them. The people that seem to have the hardest shells are often protecting an inner marshmallow that has been burned one too many times in their lives.

Unfortunately this pattern has some unintended consequences; denying those feelings is like trying to hold a beach ball under the water, eventually the ball is going to pop up in one way or another. Feelings that are buried can explode at inopportune times. I'm pretty sure that's what happened with Mom. She was trying so hard to be perfect that there were just days when she couldn't handle that pressure anymore. I know that is what happened to me when I'd snap at people. I am my mother's daughter.

Most of our addictive behaviors come from trying to cope with uncomfortable feelings. Feelings suppressed long enough also can affect our physical health. Very few of us are actually taught healthy ways of dealing with our feelings and that sweet, tender place inside. We need to acknowledge and honor the messages those feelings are sharing with us about what is happening in our life. Anger means we feel that a boundary has been violated. Sadness means we are experiencing some sort of loss. Joy—well you know what joy means, don't you? We have to feel the feeling, and embrace its secrets before we can let it go. There have been times when I made the mistake of trying to intellectualize my way out of emotion by trying to find a lesson before I've actually acknowledged the feeling. It is rather like putting a pretty covering over a toxic dump—saying, "That's okay I've learned from it," when part of me inside is screaming, "OUCH that hurts and to tell you the truth it sucks!"

When we don't acknowledge the pain we feel and stuff it down; when we make rules about which emotions are acceptable and which ones are not, we don't actually just choke off the "bad" emotions, we don't have access to our full joy either. I didn't realize what a small percentage of my joy was available to me until I set free some of the fear, anger and pain. It is a delicate dance feeling an emotion and letting it flow through you without blame or running away, and trusting that the spiritual knowing will come as you sit with it. We must lovingly be with our grief, fear or anger before we can overcome it. Honoring begins the transformation process, denial delays it. When we can experience and express our feelings without blaming or sucking others into the drama, we have made a major step toward being a conscious adult.

So how do we learn to live with this squishy, tender part that many of us are embarrassed by? I've come to believe we can embrace it and learn from it in a more adult way than throwing a tantrum or locking ourselves in a bathroom. "Feel. Embrace. Let go. Learn. Again & again," I repeat to myself as though I am counting out the steps of a dance.

I also found great help in the Buddhist meditation practice called Tonglen. It is a simple practice of breathing in what we are feeling and breathing out compassion. I do this first for myself and then for all the people in the world who are feeling what I am feeling. It seems counter-intuitive to choose to breathe in suffering, but it is in the very breathing in that I accept the suffering and stop fighting the feeling. I let the feeling wash over me, and I breathe out sending love out into the world. This is a practice of accepting that this human journey has moments that are uncomfortable. I practice to love and understand that soft, sweet, tender place inside.

The inner marshmallow allows us to connect with the heart of another — to be moved by the courage and beauty — to let our soft centers merge into oneness. It is in that communion of compassion that our souls touch. It is in those moments we really see each other. True intimacy comes from the willingness to share our feelings and witness for each other this rich and messy thing called life. Feelings are the openings through which we can learn, connect and grow. I don't want to wall up or shut down this gift of feeling. I don't want to be a person who isn't touched by life. I don't want to be a person unmoved by heartfelt emotions. Our feelings are the doorway to greater understanding of life. When we embrace the feeling part of this human journey, we experience our fullness in the world and our connection to everything in it.

> **What family patterns are you following with regard to your feelings? Are there feelings that are okay and not okay for you? Can you embrace your soft sweet tender place inside? Can you see it in others? What shifts when you practice the Tonglen meditation, accepting your feelings as you breathe in and then breathing out compassion?**

CHAPTER 7

HUSH!

Hush! Your spirit calls you to be still. Don't ignore it. You think that there are so many more important things to do. You find life isn't working, so you do more. Your energy – your spirit scatters to the wind because you keep doing – filling your calendar with activities and feeling no peace. Eating food but never satisfying the hunger in your soul. You are terrorized by the voices in your head which tell you "you aren't good enough – do more," because no matter what you do it doesn't seem to work. It is like you are flogging a beast of burden that is doing all it can do and you keep beating it and beating it until it falls down exhausted and refuses to move.

You desire peace and yet you do everything but sit still. You run from who you are. You run from stillness and acceptance. You are exhausted and yet you fight stillness because you are afraid: afraid of knowing who you are; afraid of listening to the voices in your head and heart; afraid of realizing the areas that you are hurt and separated from wholeness; afraid of the challenge of healing those hurts; afraid of admitting the times that you feel that you haven't lived up to the callings of your spirit; afraid of living from a sacred heart.

Stop. Just Stop. Stop running. Ask for help and guidance and then be very still and quiet. Stop doing and start listening. Consider the possibility that I am whispering to you all the time but you can't hear it because you are so busy. This is the surrender I ask for. When you listen to my presence inside, your body will flood with peace. You need silence so that you may hear. Stop talking, stop doing and sit now. Stop. Be Still. Hush!

~~~

"Let us be silent, that we may hear the whispers of the gods."

— Ralph Waldo Emerson

~~~

When I was a child, I thought that the Psalm *"Be still, and know that I am God,"* was Art admonishing me as a naughty child, "Be still Carol and know that I am bigger than you. I am writing down all your transgressions and I can zap you with a lightning bolt, send a flood or a plague if you aren't good. Be still because I am so powerful and you are so worthless." I believed that God was outside me and like a bully was telling me to "sit down and know that I am in charge. You will do things my way or else." Now I see that Bible verse as an invitation to go inside and listen to that Voice within. Or when I don't know what to do, to be still and ask for help from higher sources than my mind.

This idea of being still didn't come naturally to me. I fought it every step of the way like a child having that kick and scream tantrum. "I don't want to be still. I don't like it! I can't do it!" There are some people who are naturally quiet and introspective. They like to take things slow and easy. I am not one of those people. As a child I often heard "Do you have ants in your pants? Stop fidgeting, sit still!" I still tend to squirm in meetings that go on too long. I'm an extrovert. I talk with my hands and body. I used to thrive on the adrenaline of deadline pressure and the drama of too much to do in a day. Not only is it busy in my outside world, it is very busy in my head. There is The Voice, which is wise, but there are also other thoughts or voices in my head that are like a huge out-of-control committee with no rules of order — voices of judgment, worrying, planning, anticipating, and dreaming — all trying to be heard.

When I think of people who are still, I think of people who meditate. For years, I couldn't imagine a moment without busy thoughts much less comfortably sitting for meditation and chanting a mantra. The word meditation was so loaded with expectations of how I had to be while doing it. I couldn't sit in lotus position. I couldn't make my mind stop, and I wasn't sure that I wanted to. Isn't that what happens to brain-dead people? Part of me liked the idea of meditating — achieving some sort of peace from those thoughts — but another part knew it just wasn't me. It was so hard to sit still when my "to do" list was calling me.

For fifteen years while I juggled my acting career and then my hypnotherapy business and law firm work, I maintained a schedule that was packed from nine in the morning till midnight or 1 a.m. I attended many time management courses that showed me how to get more done in a day. I'd push myself relentlessly for months on end until I was so tired I needed to collapse in bed for a day and not move. If I ignored the message to slow down, I would get bronchitis or the flu and then have no choice but to rest.

When I started my own business I thought I'd have more flexibility—what I found was that I had the worst boss I'd ever had. She had unrealistic expectations. She was saying, "Why isn't that done yet?" Waking me up in the middle of the night nagging me about what needed to happen next. When I finally realized this I had to fire the bad boss and look for a kinder more compassionate one. My goal was to find the balance between doing and taking time for myself, to create a life of meaningful doing—not just being busy.

I know my relationship with stillness started to shift when I began to study acting. Through acting I was introduced to forms of stillness that had a purpose. Hypnosis helped me to program my mind to dream a character into being and be less nervous in auditions. I was introduced to Julia Cameron's book, *The Artist's Way*,[6] which contained exercises for recovering your connection to your creativity. I loved the process she called "morning pages," which was sitting first thing in the morning and writing three pages long hand of everything that came to mind without stopping or censoring. I seldom did my writing first thing in the morning, so I called the process my "brain dump." I simply set a timer for fifteen minutes or agreed to write at least three pages long hand and then wrote down everything that came into my brain without censoring. Writing was comfortable for me. It became a form of meditative thought watching— seeing those thoughts spill out onto the paper helped me stay

---

[6] Julia Cameron, *The Artist's Way, A Spiritual Path to Higher Creativity*, ©1992, 2002 Julie Cameron, Jeremy P. Tarcher/Putnam

in the moment. This automatic writing became a practice I enjoyed but started and stopped again and again. It was the process that called to me on that day in April 2008 that began the process of writing this book.

In those months that followed, the message "Be still!" kept appearing on the page again and again. I was sitting down to listen and write every day. What more did The Voice want? My whole life had been about achieving and then never truly being able to appreciate the achievement before I moved on to the next thing. If I was busy, I wouldn't have to acknowledge the things I feared. If I kept running around, I wouldn't have to notice that life was calling to me to make changes; that there was a conversation that needed to happen or that something was broken that needed my attention. I thought I could avoid the fears by being busy. But underneath, the fear was churning and requiring me to stay busy so I wouldn't face it. I didn't want to hear "be still" but like a child who is overtired and needs to sleep, it was exactly what I needed.

One day it occurred to me that perhaps I needed to forget about my expectations of what meditation looked like to others and to find a way of being still that worked for me. I decided to call it quiet time. I played soothing instrumental music and sat in my big overstuffed chair. Here were my rules for quiet time: Stay in the chair for fifteen minutes with my eyes closed, listen to the music and breathe. No falling asleep! That was it! I adjusted my body position if I needed to. I didn't worry about a little fidget. I set the intention to slow down and see if I could find this illusive stillness everyone talked about. I didn't judge where my mind went. In fact, I let the voices in my head go to town. I didn't try to stifle or stop them. "Do your worst," I'd tell them as I closed my eyes. I kept a journal by the chair and when I was done with my time out, I'd spend another ten-to-fifteen minutes writing down whatever those voices were saying.

Funny, when I gave them the opportunity to speak, without judgment, they were like a committee of workers that no one ever took seriously and now finally had the boss's ear. At first, they had a lot to say and all were talking at once, but once I patiently listened to each aspect of me as it spoke and noticed each thought, I realized they simply wanted me to be loved and safe. Certain voices repeated old thought patterns that were no longer helpful, others pointed to wounds from the past that I hadn't dealt with. The more I listened to the voices and truly heard them, the more they were willing to wait their turn. I felt more peaceful and centered. Like so many people I thought I couldn't meditate because it was busy in my head. I didn't realize that perhaps one of the reasons it was busy is that I never really listened to or delved deeper into the reason why those voices needed to be heard. When I was silent long enough to let them have their say and tire, it was then that my higher soul voices could speak. The voices of spirit are often hidden by the louder voices of fear and doubt.

After six months of sitting with the music, I realized I could sit—just me and the chair—and breathe. And I'd actually have moments of that peace or nothingness that others talked about when they talk about meditation. For two years I preferred sitting to music, then one day it shifted and I preferred silence. I have a meditation practice that I call my adult "time out." I don't sit still easily. I move and shift around quite often. My goal is simply to create the space where a connection can happen. Some days in my stillness, I achieve those blank spaces where I just am—me and the chair. Some days I have a hard time not falling asleep, some days I have hard time sitting still, some days it feels like coming home and other days it feels like I have to face my deepest ugliest self. And most days I still have to force myself to show up and do it.

When I talk to friends and clients, I find many people have an uncomfortable relationship with stillness, silence and not doing. There is relief in knowing I am not alone in this ambivalent relationship with meditation. When one of my co-workers at the law firm asked me what some of the things I was learning were as I worked on this book, I told him that it is essential to learn to be still. He looked at me and asked, "Does sleeping count?" I laughed. "No it doesn't." He said that he had a hard time with stillness. "You are one of those people who meditate," he said. "I can't do it. I just can't sit still!" I laughed as I explained to him the uneasy truce I have made with stillness.

I wouldn't be writing this book if I hadn't slowed down and gotten quiet enough to listen. I wouldn't have heard the Lessons, nor would I have reflected about what they meant to me if I didn't intentionally carve out the time to be still. I grew up being taught prayers to say and I spent a lot of time asking God for things. It was a rather one-sided relationship. I did all the talking and I never was quiet enough to receive or listen. This Voice of the soul and the sacred speaks in a whisper, intuition or impulse. "Be still" is the invitation to go inward, to take time to be present in order to hear those whispers and find the love and joy.

Like those people who change their diet and then want to tell you how bad the food that you are eating is; I want to shout out to the world, "We all have to take time to be still. It is essential to connecting to the Sacred in you and in the world. You don't have to meditate in anyone else's way. Experiment and find a way of being still that works for you. And no, watching TV and sleeping do not count!" Maybe you are one of those people for whom traditional meditation works. Great! But if you aren't, perhaps you need to trick your mind like I did and say, "I'm not meditating I'm just sitting still listening to music." Or, "I'm not meditating. I'm just sitting quietly in nature noticing everything that goes on around me." Or, "I'm not meditating. I'm just paying attention to every step I take and being present on my walk for the next ten minutes." Because it isn't whether you can get deep into nothingness like a Zen monk, it is about whether you are willing to give yourself time to slow down enough to open the channel of connection and start listening.

And when you think you can't be still, believe me, I understand. I've found that the most important word to say to myself when life gets hectic and I am overwhelmed, or when I sit to be still and my mind is so busy that I can't seem to find the pause button, is, "Hush." I say that word over and over again to myself like a mantra; gently, lovingly again and again. I speak to myself like I'm talking to a baby who is tired but just can't settle down and rest: Hush. Hushhhhhhh. Hush. Hush.

> **What keeps you from slowing down & being still? Can you find a way to give yourself quiet time that is tailored for you? Hush. Slow down and listen. Hush.**

CHAPTER 8

THE WELL & SPIRITUAL HYGIENE

You thirst for meaning and connection, yet you put off going to the well. You say you don't have time. And then when you finally decide to nurture yourself, you take a thimble – allow yourself a small sip – a miserly amount. Your consciousness is in drought. It is a dry dusty landscape when you try to define meaning from the world of things and achievements; when you focus on all the problems; when you are determined to see with eyes of judgment.

Trying to make your life work using only the smaller human self and not the spirit within is exhausting. You are looking for things outside to fill you and have forgotten that the connection to your sacred self – the Divine within is the place where all your thirsts are quenched. Tending to this spiritual self is essential.

The well of Consciousness of Absolute Love, Beauty and Truth is yours. How often will you go to the well? How often will you forget to drink? Are you waiting for someone else to fill your cup?

No one else can. Go to the well and drink of the cup of kindness, love and connection – Fill yourself. Practice bridging the ordinary with the extraordinary and claim the peace that is yours.

~~~

"When the well's dry, we know the worth of water." —Benjamin Franklin

~~~

As a child, I hated getting up on Sunday mornings. Mom and Dad made sure my sister Luanne and I never missed Sunday mass, even if it meant sending our dog Tippie in to lick our faces or turning up the stereo with loud music to get us out of bed.

For them, it was a time to nurture their connection with spirit; for me on the other hand, it was time to daydream about donuts while I went through the motions of the mass—standing, kneeling, sitting—reciting the prayers like a robot—killing time until breakfast. You see, you were supposed to have not eaten for a full hour before you received communion. The body of Christ could not mix with Cheerios™. And since I barely rolled out of bed in time to dress for church, I would sit in church contemplating the donuts we would buy on the way home. Did I want a Bismarck with jelly or a chocolate covered Long John? There was one priest who could say the whole mass with a homily and serve a hundred or more people communion in about twenty-five minutes. I loved when that priest said mass!

On Saturdays when we were on family vacations, my parents would open the phone book in the hotel room and look for where the Catholic Church was so that we could go to mass on Sunday. Or they'd ask at restaurants, "Where's the nearest Catholic Church?" I was always embarrassed. But my parents had the rule: church on Sunday was not optional. We might be on vacation but we weren't missing mass.

In the years after I left home, I didn't give much thought to how important regular time for my spiritual self was. I prayed when I needed help and kept gratitude lists to remind myself that life was essentially good. I read books, went to workshops, dropped in on church services and developed my own form of meditation, reflection and writing. But I wasn't consistent. I'd say I wanted a deeper connection to meaning and purpose, to my intuition, to a more personal relationship with whatever the higher power was, but I often didn't make the time to show up for those spiritual activities. In fact, they were the activities that often got crossed off my list on a busy day.

When I made the commitment to listen and write every day, it was non-negotiable for about six months; then it became easier to take The Voice and the experience for granted and to let days go by in between meditations and writing sessions. I'd find myself exhausted and emotionally down. "What is wrong with me?" I'd think. I went over everything that had happened in my life and could see nothing wrong. So I'd head back to the journal and my quiet time to see what I could figure out. As soon as I sank into the quiet time it became clear—the only thing that was wrong was I forgot to show up for this spiritual part of myself.

Finally after several of these "a-ha moments," I realized I needed to change my thinking about spiritual time. I thought back to an experience that I had when I moved to Los Angeles in the late 1980s. When I first got to LA, I only knew two people, Jim, a friend from college and his girlfriend (now wife), Cheryl. I couldn't depend on them for my whole social life so I decided I needed to reach out and ask people to do things with me. One day at my new job, I overheard one of the women saying that it was so hard to make friends in Los Angeles. A couple of days later, I asked her if she had plans for lunch, and whether she wanted to go grab something together. She said, "That sounds good, how about a week from Tuesday?" I thought, *A week from Tuesday is fine but I am hungry today.* We never did have lunch together. A week from Tuesday came and she had to postpone. We rescheduled several times but she always had a reason why today wasn't a good day for lunch. It occurred to me that I now knew why she didn't have a lot of friends. So, often I'm like that co-worker, bemoaning the fact that I don't feel at peace and don't feel happy or healthy and meanwhile doing very little to make that connection happen. When I am still, I connect to peace and often get guidance. Even though I know it works for me, I fight it. I put it off. I try to kid myself that it is optional or that it can wait. This is sort of a "Duh!" realization, but connecting with my sacred self requires the discipline of showing up on a regular basis.

I may have followed a different spiritual path than my parents. But I have to thank them for modeling for me the importance of committing to spiritual practice. If I want to see my life as a sacred journey, then why would I stop doing the very things that have been showing me the way? I remember the first time I was in a car with a GPS system. I was riding in my friend Julie's car on the freeway and we passed the exit that we were supposed to take. The GPS spoke out in the male British voice she had selected, "recalculating," and proceeded to give us new directions from the next exit. I laughed to myself, "If only it could be that simple for other 'wrong turns' we take in life!" Then I had a big "Aha!" Time committed to a spiritual practice such as quiet time to consciously listen to my heart and The Voice within is like connecting with a GPS that helps me stay connected with my sacred self. When I feel out of sorts and I sit down quietly, it is almost like my internal guidance is calling out, "recalculating," and trying to find the way to my spirit. Perhaps this time could be called my God Positioning System. It points me in the direction of the highest form of myself and what I need to know.

I've got to regularly nourish my connection with Spirit, Source and my most authentic self to feel the flow of life around me. It can't be the thing I cross off my list when life gets busy. It has to be the thing that I wouldn't consider leaving the house without taking care of — sort of like brushing my teeth or taking a shower. I don't really think about whether I like these personal hygiene tasks, I just do them because they are good for me and people don't want me out in the world without showering or brushing my teeth. And I now know that I don't want to venture out in the world without having taken some time to connect with the sacred within. I need spiritual hygiene time each day as much as I need a shower! When I don't sit for quiet time, I go through my day like a balloon that someone untied the knot from — hurriedly moving from one thing to the next until all the air is gone and I am exhausted. I look back and see all the moments that I wasn't fully present. Going to the well isn't just about being still and meditating, it is about how well I nourish and take care of myself — body, mind and spirit.

It is a special kind of self-care to give ourselves time with that soul or heart space that connects us to meaning and purpose and helps us stay balanced. It can't be negotiable. It reminds us that we are connected to something bigger than the immediate circumstances of our lives. It is what we practice, not what we preach, that determines the quality of our existence. If we want to fully participate in our time here on earth in human form as spirit, we have to create time each day to allow the music of spirit to guide us. The well of Consciousness of Absolute Love, Beauty and Truth is ours if we are willing to show up and drink from it.

> **How are you at making regular time to take care of your spirit? Do you need to go to the well more often? What helps you to remember love?**

CHAPTER 9

WHAT IF THIS MOMENT IS PERFECT?

Ask yourself: "What if this moment is perfect?" This moment that you are whining about, those people that you are irritated with — what if — you trusted that there is no problem? Questioned your assumptions? Detached from your opinions? What if you didn't have to have it all figured out? What if you didn't judge something that happened to you as right or wrong or good or bad? What if it just was? What if you were more interested in how many ways you could look at something than falling into the trap of certainty?

What if you just said, "I don't know; I'm making this up as I go along?" What if you were willing to be foolish? What if you were willing to live the mystery rather than solve it? What if you were willing to love whole-heartedly but were also willing to let go and trust that whatever seemed like a betrayal or hurt was not what it appeared? Nothing happens to you. It all happens for you. Trust this.

Being spiritual will not give you a free pass to a life without pain. Sometimes there is hardship so that you will face your fears and grow. Learn to see through the pain to the gifts and lessons within. Everything that happens to you is perfect. Everything. It is sent from your highest self and the Universe so that you can see the results of what you have created in the past or what you need to learn today. You co-create. Perhaps you need to change course, look deeper, love more. You create the meaning to the events of your life. It is up to you to decide whether you will blossom from the conditions you are experiencing here, move to a higher state of awareness or whether you will stay here, complain, stagnate and fight. It is up to you to grow in love or choose to turn away. I keep inviting you to love and give you endless opportunities to see the path. I light candles and torches to light your way. You can choose to follow the path or you can walk in the dark. It is up to you. The meaning to every discomfort is there inside. Your sacred self is waiting for you to choose growth and living over staying safe and hiding from your evolution as a strong and beautiful spirit warrior.

What if you put down the "shoulds" of judgment and accepted and trusted now? What if you let love and your spirit run the show? You are part of the Divine order. Let yourself flow with me. In me, there is no separation. In me, there is no shortage of time, no lack. Detach from the way it is supposed to be and live now free in spirit and trust that this moment is perfect and your spirit is guiding you exactly as it should.

~~~

"This very moment is the perfect teacher, and lucky for us, it's with us wherever we are." —Pema Chödrön

~~~

Perfection has always been a slippery concept for me. I tried to be perfect but knew I wasn't. I was human. This spiritual understanding that everything is perfect—that the universe is conspiring on my behalf was hard to hang on to. Even though part of me knew that everything I was experiencing was probably for my greater good, I wanted to argue that things weren't perfect. "There's a war going on. There are people starving. There are women who live in countries where they are attacked for expressing themselves. I just pulled money out of savings so I could pay my bills. Two clients cancelled this week. My mom's health is failing and I feel guilty about not being able to help out with her care. And I've been trying to write this fricking chapter for over a week and it won't come together. The world is not perfect," I wrote as, my mind and heart raged. But the quiet Voice persisted and asked, *But what if this moment is perfect?* I felt like a petulant child and found myself saying, "But it isn't!" The Voice replied *What if it is?*

I started to think about the idea of perfect moments. I know I have experienced perfect moments in life:

- Being in the delivery room with my friend Judy and watching her daughter Ellin enter the world.

- Sitting at the Hollywood Bowl under the stars listening to Etta James sing "At Last" with my head on the shoulder of a man I loved.

- Looking out the window of the apartment I rented in Paris for vacation, gazing at the Eiffel Tower all lit up and realizing that I actually was in Paris, somewhere I dreamed of being for years.

But today was not like any of those moments—it didn't feel perfect. The Voice asked me to look for other perfect moments. The ones I missed at the time but now see how perfect they were. Okay. I gave it a shot.

- Buying fresh cherries in Michigan and spitting pits out the window as we drove across the state on a family vacation.
- Playing Scrabble™ on Sunday nights with my mom and dad and sister.
- Singing as a family in church.
- Family reunion picnics at Lawler Park on the Mississippi in Prairie du Chien, Wisconsin with my cousins.
- The time my high school friend Sally helped me dig my parents' car out of a snow drift, using rugs for traction, shovels and lots of swearing and laughter, to avoid hearing the "I told you so" from Mom & Dad.
- Laughing with my sister about what I did on my vacation—laying cove in her kitchen (a home improvement project—not a sex act!)—and having my mom smile and call us her giggly girls even though we were in our thirties.
- A wonderfully simple New Year's Eve with that man I was in love with cooking together and enjoying each other's company.
- A drive along the beach at sunset.
- Watching the Foo Fighters play some of my favorite songs in an acoustic set at the Forum when a friend got me in on the floor right next to the stage.
- That night at the Viper Room watching Lovehammers play. (Yes, music is often part of my perfect moments. There are times where the music is so perfect it is like God is giving me a soundtrack for my life.)

This list of perfect moments was actually easy to come up with, and I realized most of them were never consciously acknowledged as perfect moments until I wrote this list. Then I thought of the moments that seemed awful at the time that turned out to be for the best in the end.

- Losing my father at twenty-six, which gave me time to heal my relationship with my mother and see her for the amazing woman she is.

- Breaking up with that lovely man because I realized that we really wanted different things and it was time for me to move on.

- The year as a manager under pressure to do more with less, lay off employees and take on other departments as other managers quit or were laid off; because of this difficult year, I finally gave myself permission to follow my heart and pursue my acting dream.

- Failing to break through and become a full-time working actor, which led to me studying hypnotherapy and to the spiritual journey that I am on today.

- Filing bankruptcy; this led me to find out that I had a hole in my spirit that I was trying to fill with things and also showed me who my friends were. They loved and supported me even though I had made this mistake.

So many tough moments and experiences now seem absolutely perfect in retrospect. As painful as they were, I wouldn't trade away the learning I got from them for anything.

But is this moment, "perfect"? I hear the whisper, *"Sweetie, this moment is all you have. Don't judge it or waste it."* When I hear news of an unexpected death, I wake up and realize life is short. There are no guarantees. But it doesn't take long to go back into the coma of everyday life, numbed by routine—unaware of the preciousness that is now. But still, it is a challenge to look at some of the tragedies in the world without thinking about the way we want it to be. It is so tempting to rail against the Universe or God and say, "Why would you do something like that?"

When my nieces were young and they were served an unfamiliar food, they'd screw up their faces and say, "I don't like it," before they even tried it. How many times am I like them, reacting to things that are different or unknown with the same sort of judgment? Rather than trying to understand it and experience it, I judge first.

"What if this moment is perfect?" The key part of that question is the *"what if."* *What if* I assume this moment is perfect even if I can't quite see it yet? *What if* something different than I thought is going on here? I know from my hypnotherapy and coaching practice that if I don't ask the right questions, I can't help the client find their answers. What if there were better questions that I could ask myself? What if I used this moment to look at the world with eyes of love? What if I used this moment to act with love for myself and others? What if I did the best I could in this moment and let everything else go? What if I look for the perfection in what I can do, rather than griping about what I perceive as wrong? What if I'm simply curious about what this might mean rather than deciding right now that I know it isn't right?

Inspired by this thought, I decided to give it a try to see if I could look at everything as though it were perfect. What would happen if I tried to see everything in the way God saw it? I was heading out on a walk with Sadie and vowed to try to see everything on that walk through the eyes of love and perfection. It was almost as though I had taken some sort of drug. The colors of the flowers were brighter and the petals more distinct. I saw a tree that had a scar from where a branch came off in a storm, and my first thought was, "that must have hurt!" I noticed the tree had been wounded and yet was still fully alive and beautiful. If I could see it in that tree, I could start to look for that same dignity in people. I felt compassion for the woman so caught up in living in a big city that she couldn't even make eye contact as we passed on the sidewalk. I spoke to other people I had been in the same neighborhood with for ten years and had never introduced myself to. I laughed more robustly at the way Sadie doesn't like to walk on the grass unless it is time to "go potty." There was so much beauty and connection on that walk that I came home inspired and almost vibrating with the beauty of the world.

But I couldn't hold onto the lightness for long; an hour or so back at home and it was gone. The day-to-day reality of life's tasks took over. But there was something big in that experience that reminded me that, just like meditation is a practice, I can train myself to find something perfect in every experience. It is a choice. I can be the Pollyanna or the pessimist.

If we train ourselves to notice the perfection, even in things that seem far from perfect, we are choosing the type of world we want to live in—a world that says, "yes!" to life.

Stuck in traffic? I can be mad about something I can't control or I can say, "I guess I was supposed to have more time in my car to think." A client cancels his appointment; I choose to believe that the Universe is giving me more time to write rather than that he is screwing up my day. As I practice looking for the perfection in everything, most times I find it. There still are things that cause me to cry out, "This is so wrong, it can't be perfect," and I've learned to ask the Universe to show me what I am missing.

If all we have is this moment, then it is the perfect moment to practice accepting what is. This moment is the perfect moment to learn to love ourselves and our world with all its contradictions. It is a perfect moment to let spirit run the show. It is the perfect moment to remember to trust. It is the perfect moment to look at what we can do right now. If we see something that we don't like in the world, this moment is the perfect moment for us to see what we can do to make that thing better.

Maybe I can't feed all the starving children in the world but I can donate money to feed several. Maybe I can't solve all the injustices in the world, but in this moment I can deal with being less judgmental about a friend or family member. How can I be more loving and closer to my highest self in this moment? This moment is the perfect moment to be sacred no matter what I am seeing with my human eyes, no matter what I fear. What if this moment is divine? What if it is just up to me to choose to see it that way? And if something needs to change, what if this moment is perfect in showing me what I need to do to allow that change to happen?

Create a list of your perfect moments. Can you think of the moments that didn't seem perfect to begin with but now looking at them you can see the perfection in them? Practice walking through the world looking at things with the eyes of God. What shifts for you?

CHAPTER 10

THE RULES OF EVIDENCE

You are not your stories. They are just reflections of who you think you are. You are not the snapshots frozen in time from yesterday. You have chosen these illusions you live by. Look to your past and notice where you have left part of your soul behind — any story you tell of not being whole. You've given your power to an event that today is just a story. It no longer exists. Forgive yourself, forgive the other. Call your soul back with love. Move on.

Look at your stories but don't live there. Let your stories inform your life with love, align you with the light or throw them all away. You select the evidence that proves your truths. You can look for the ways you are connected with the sacred or find evidence of why you should be scared. You are supported or you are lacking. It is your choice. When you identify with your "scared-ness" your world is scary. It is not your world that needs fixing; it is the mind and heart that has you seeing the world as anything less than a sacred space where you can create. There is evidence all around you of interconnectedness – that there is no "we" or "me," only Divine One. When you live from your sacredness, the world blossoms in beauty and love. You collectively choose the world you will inhabit.

What do you need to prove that sacred love is most powerful? That you are supported? What do you need? Are you even looking for that evidence? Each minute, there are a thousand ways that show you I am, but you choose to look hard for all the ways I am not.

You are so creative you can find evidence and twist it to prove whatever point you desire. You can choose to be right and make others wrong. Think again. Does it help you live in peace? These moral thoughts about what and who is right and wrong, do they help you get close to me? To others? To see the interconnectedness of all? Could you accept that most rights and wrongs are just distractions that keep you from love? Look at your evidence gathering and ask yourself, "Is this love?" If you are judging, condemning or making yourself better or worse than – that is not love.

You only have to ask and I will begin to heal your perceptions and bring you back to the most sacred perception of your world. Ask me to help you believe in love with your mind so that your heart can expand and grow. Ask me to help you see the evidence of the love that is all around you.

~~~

"If you change the way you look at things, the things you look at change."

—Wayne Dyer

~~~

I spent over 25 years of my life working in law firms and became very familiar with the rules of evidence that govern how information can be obtained and how it can be used in court. I have spent many long hours with attorneys reviewing millions of pages of paper. In all those pages, there were all sorts of stories that could be told. Crafting an argument for court was a matter of assembling the evidence that supported your story. Each side in a dispute has its version of the truth as it was seen through their perspective. The outcome of any litigation was not always "the truth" — just a version of the truth or a compromise that worked or in some cases was a totally human miscarriage of justice.

In the early 1990s, I was an alternate on a jury for a man accused of felony murder — murder committed during the commission of a crime. As an alternate, I did not get to deliberate, and I was stunned when the jury returned a guilty verdict. The defendant looked like someone I wouldn't want to meet in an alley, but the testimony linking him to the crime scene was so thin, I couldn't believe that others thought he was guilty. I saw a reasonable doubt opening that you could drive a truck through: the eye witness had been no closer than fifteen-to-twenty feet away from the person holding the gun. This same witness had been in the bar drinking for four-to-five hours before the incident, hadn't been wearing his glasses and had initially described the gunman as a light-skinned Latino man. Sitting in front of me was a tall Caucasian man, who looked like he might belong in Hell's Angels but didn't look Latino to me at all. When asked by the defense why the witness picked this man out of the line up — the witness said, "He looked like someone who *could* have done it." Not "he looked like the man who did it." There was nothing else linking this man to the crime. In my mind — an easy not guilty, and yet twelve other people believed that witness and were happy to have the "dangerous man" off the street.

The defendant cried out when the verdict was read, "You are wrong. God help you, you are wrong!" I had nightmares about that case for weeks afterward. There was nothing I could do. I was an alternate. I hoped his attorney was able to help him on appeal. The case has stuck with me on a visceral level ever since. It reminded me that our experiences and opinions color the way we view our world. Twelve other jurors came to a completely different conclusion, all based on the same evidence. They saw the evidence in a completely different light than I did.

We are doing this insidious filtering of information and building our cases in our personal lives. It is there in our discussions of politics. It is there in our relationships with our family. We wonder, "How could that other person look at what I see and believe something totally different than I do?"

The Voice asks: *"How do you want to tell your life story – as the triumphant hero/heroine's journey or a victim's horror story?"* It is all about what evidence we use to craft our stories. There is so much power in how we filter and collect evidence and yet most of us don't think twice before we launch into a story about something that happened to us. We don't realize that we have many options in how we tell our story and the option we choose insidiously colors our lives to the point of becoming what we think is true.

One day, I was walking Sadie and a man with two huge Irish Wolfhound-like dogs was approaching from the opposite direction on the sidewalk. Since it looked like he was having a hard time controlling the grey and black horse-sized dogs, Sadie and I stepped out onto the street to pass them. In an instant before I could do anything, I was standing in the middle of a dog fight. I could hear Sadie under the two bigger dogs; growling, yelping and squeaking as she was fighting back with all her might but clearly being overpowered. Frozen, my heart pounded as I looked at the leash in my hand with Sadie's collar hanging off the end of it. Somehow she had slipped out of her collar.

The dog walker tried to grab the big dogs but he couldn't move them. A Latino man in his thirties in a pickup truck pulled over, crossing lanes of traffic to get to us, honking his horn and jumping out of the truck with something club-like his hands. (I honestly can't recall what exactly he had—a baseball bat or a stick. It was all a blur.) The two men were able to get the dogs off of Sadie and shoo them down the street. Sadie was yelping out in that high-pitched noise that no dog owner who loves her dog as much as I love mine wants to hear. As I shakily ran my hands over her body, certain that I was going to find blood, I only found that she was covered in saliva slobber. Thankfully the bigger dogs were trying to dominate, not kill. I repeatedly told her and myself, "You are okay. We are okay."

I put on Sadie's collar and started to coax her to walk down the street so that we could get away in case the dogs came back. I heard a man yell, "Are you alright?" It was the dog walker, a thin thirty-something man with long hair in a ponytail and tattoos on his arms. "The dogs are in their house and can't hurt you!" We sat on a curb of the driveway of a nearby church parking lot. "I'm so sorry! Is she okay?" He sat down and started to pet Sadie. "Their leashes snapped! I should have told the owner they needed stronger leashes. It was my fault." He explained that he had only been walking those dogs for a couple of weeks and didn't know them well. I looked at him and realized he was also shaking and said, "We are all fine. It is okay." He continued to pet Sadie saying, "I'm sorry, little girl. You were so brave protecting your mama, weren't you?"

I could decide that walking my dog was dangerous. I could be mad that someone would be walking 100-pound dogs with leashes that wouldn't hold them. I could stay scared or I could choose to look at how fortunate we were. Neither Sadie nor I got hurt. Amazing strangers, my angel in the pickup truck and this kind dog walker, had courageously jumped in to help and look after us. I was fortunate. We truly were okay.

A day or so later, a friend of mine said to me, "Carol, it was probably fortunate that you were the one there when the leashes snapped. Not a small child or someone who would be traumatized for a long time. Now the dog walker will get them stronger leashes." I hadn't thought of that. I was just happy that I didn't have to make a trip to the emergency vet for Sadie or the emergency room for me. Another friend got more caught up in the drama of what had happened, and said, "I would be scarred for life!" It really is a choice in how we hold the stories of what happens to us in life, isn't it?

Living sacred means collecting evidence of all the ways love works in the world, choosing to craft our stories with the highest viewpoint and perhaps even letting go of the need for stories completely. I take another lesson from Sadie. She was able to shake off what had happened and be her loving, confident self within a few blocks. While I hung onto the story, she has long forgotten it.

Each day we gather evidence and craft stories about the events in our lives. It is time to choose those stories more consciously. What evidence are we collecting? "How our world supports us?" or "How is life not working?" Are we defined by our fears or our connection to the Divine? The evidence we collect will prove our case and attract more of the same. If we are constantly training ourselves to see whether we are ahead of someone else and what is missing in our lives, or if we collect evidence of how we are not good enough, or see all the ways the Universe isn't there for us, we will be successful at building that case. If we believe that story to be true, we may find ourselves tired and scared before we even begin the day.

If, on the other hand, we look for the ways we are supported, the helpful coincidences that spring up unexpectedly, the friends or strangers who step in when we need them, the unexpected cash that shows up just in time, then we see growing evidence of support and possibilities for our lives.

What we focus on, we attract. Maybe more important to remember, what we focus on, we see. We miss the good stuff if we are focusing on the bad. It is a choice. Life may be giving us 100 reasons to be unhappy or scared today, but we can choose to find at least 101 reasons to be happy and live from our hearts. Each day, choosing the evidence and stories that align us with that loving sacred connection is the most powerful thing we can do.

> **Are you collecting evidence to support a world view inconsistent with what you want in life? Are you focusing on how life doesn't work? Or how it does? What stories are you hanging onto that no longer serve you or hold you back? Would it be more helpful to let those stories go?**

CHAPTER 11

GETTING PAST THE LIES

Come out of hiding. The world doesn't need you to lie. Don't be offended. I am not trying to shame or embarrass you. I want you to blossom forth in all your beauty. The biggest deceptions are the ones you tell yourself. You may think you are being truthful but there are layers you need to break through. Layers of self-deception where you think your story is the true you. Layers of deception in a society that refuses to see what is most important and real, that fights over positions rather than connecting with the best for all. When you are upset at someone else's dishonesty – see that it only holds a light up for all the ways you have lied – in words, by omission or by thinking the story is you – all the ways that you have bought into the lie that anything other than love is important.

Stand in the light and begin to see and acknowledge all the ways you delude yourself with denial. The ways politeness demands that you tell a half-truth. The ways you skirt the truth to avoid conflict. The ways you tell less than the truth because it is easier and more convenient. The deception runs so deep. Would you be willing to truly admit everything that scares you? Every time you have an ugly thought? Would you admit all the times you lie to yourself about what you are capable of doing and tell yourself—"I can't" when what you really mean is "I'm scared and don't want to fail. I don't want to be the most beautiful, powerful amazing me!" Would you admit all the times you blame someone else for stealing your light when you have freely given it away? Would you take 100% responsibility for your life? Stop hiding. Stop cowering. Be brave enough to be vulnerable. Be brave enough to be lovingly blunt with yourself. Be honest about all the things you need to strip away before you begin to criticize another. Are you willing to be totally naked? Totally vulnerable? Totally you? Look to yourself. Be brave enough to question everything you believe and hold it to the light of love.

Every lie you perceive in the outside world is just a symptom of the biggest lie of all—that you are separate. You are confused and unplugged from source and forget that you are connected to everyone. You all have forgotten who you are and fear you are not worthy of the light. Have compassion. See with love. See beneath the stories to the light inside. Love yourself enough to know that you are beautiful and do not need to cover up or hide.

~~~

"If you do not tell the truth about yourself, you cannot tell it about other people." —Virginia Woolf

~~~

I heard that childhood taunt, "Liar, liar pants on fire!" in my head as I was taking down this message. Ouch! It hurts to be called a liar. It hurts even more to admit that The Voice is right. I have a decision to make as I write this chapter. How vulnerable am I willing to be? My stomach is fluttering and my throat constricting. I feel like a spotlight has just been shined on me. I want to hide. I feel like I will have to walk around with a scarlet L on my chest — "L" for liar, "L" for loser, and I keep hearing that 1980s song in my head, "Lies, lies, lies."[7]

"Is it your practice, Ms. Woodliff, to lie to clients of the firm?" November 2001: I was sitting in a deposition and that question was asked of me. I had told a former client of the firm that we would get his ten-year-old file for him when he showed up in the office one busy Friday afternoon eighteen months earlier. I had looked up the client number for the file and based on its age I told him that the file would be off-site and we'd have to order it to be delivered. Later in the day, I remembered that firm also had some files on another floor and in an email to the records department said, the file might be on the ninth floor. I asked the records department to order the file. "You said it was off-site—why did you tell him that if you knew it could be on the ninth floor?" Problem was after the fact, we couldn't locate the file. I had indicated we'd order a file based on the fact that a file number existed. Normally when a file number existed there were files— everything generated paper.

In trying to be helpful I made it seem like getting the file would be easy, an assumption I made that didn't turn out to be true. So while my intentions were good, my execution had been less than 100% in alignment with the truth. I should have said, "I don't know," rather than assuming information I didn't have or speculating on how things might work. My recollection of the conversation that led to me sitting in that

---

[7] Lies, Lies, Lies by ©1982 The Thompson Twins, Thomas Bailey, Alannah Joy Currie, Joseph Martin Leeway.

deposition room was not completely clear. I hadn't intended any harm. I had been trying to help. It was a short conversation on a busy day. I thought I said that I had located the file number and we would order the file, had I misspoke? Did I tell him that I had located the file itself as he claimed?

At the break of the deposition, the client stepped into the elevator with me and my attorney and screamed at me. My lawyer had to step between me and the client in the elevator as the man advanced toward me, coming closer and closer in that tight space. That moment was a turning point in my life. As scary as it was, it turned out to be a blessing.

In the months after the deposition, I did some deep soul searching and could see that I had a pattern of being less than truthful in many areas of my life—most of the time stemming from trying to be nice to people and telling them what they wanted to hear to avoid conflict. Did this start in the confession line in the third grade? It was a pattern so habitual that I didn't even see it until I got called on it in this very painful way. Sometimes I made people happy but I'm sure other times people thought I was a two-faced bitch. They were being generous. I wanted to please so much that I was twisting myself into a person of many faces, definitely more than two! And the person I was most deceptive with was me.

I sacrificed my truth to please other people. I lied to protect myself. I lied to avoid a conflict. I lied to avoid taking total responsibility for my life. I lied to myself about my reasons for lying. I lied because it just seemed more convenient to do so. There were the social lies: "I'm sorry I can't make your party—I have a previous engagement;"

instead of, "I've been working really hard this week and the thing that would be the best for me is staying home with a good book" or, "I'm not much of a drinker and your parties tend to be wilder than I am." There are the avoidance lies: He: "What's wrong?" Me: "Nothing!" (Yeah right! I either couldn't put the words to what was wrong yet, or I was thinking if I have the conversation right now it is going to take more energy than I have, or I don't really know whether it is worth bringing up, or I was afraid he wouldn't love me if I told him my petty reason for being upset. Or maybe I just liked torturing him with my silence.) There were self-protection lies: "I have a doctor's appointment and will be late." (Actually I had a job interview, but it was probably not wise to tell the boss that!).

There are many studies that show that eye witness identification is not very reliable but still we hold what we remember seeing as truth. We have to acknowledge that the mind is a tricky thing. Even when we think we are being truthful, we may not be factual. Our minds like to see what is in alignment with our world view — that evidence thing I talked about in the previous chapter. I've made up stories about why people do the things they do, assigning motives based on my assumptions. On my most judgmental day, the people who belong to that political party are greedy or heartless. He is not paying attention to me because he doesn't care about me.

As I write down all these admissions, a twisted part of my ego says other people don't do this. I'm bad. In fact, I'm exceptionally bad. I'm the worst liar there ever was and I'd better hide that from everyone because no one will like me if I reveal this to the world. While I was struggling over whether to include this chapter, I attended a workshop by Bryon Katie, founder of The Work, author of *Loving What Is* and several other books. Katie was working in front of the group with a woman who was angry at her ex-husband. The woman said, "He said I was a liar and a fake!" Katie looked at the woman and asked, "Are you?" The woman squirmed uncomfortably in her chair. Then Katie looked out at the audience and said, "Who here has never been a liar or a fake?" Not one person in the over 300 people attending raised his or her hand and titters of uncomfortable laughter broke out around the room. Obviously, I am not alone.

We can convince ourselves that lying can be for a good cause. And sometimes it may be. The people who hid Jews during World War II and lied to the Nazis certainly had excellent motives. I can't say that my motivations have always been that pure and noble. I'm skeptical when someone claims he or she never lies or has never lied. There may be a few paragons out there but I sincerely doubt those who won't admit to at least skirting the truth at times or telling a convenient white lie.

As much as I was told it was important to tell the truth as a child, I also got the message that my truth wasn't okay. I'd blurt out something honest but embarrassing. "She is really fat!" And I'd be shushed, "Don't say that, it's not nice!" "But it's true!" I would insist and Mom would reply, "But it's not nice to say that!" It happened enough times that I got the message. Certain thoughts and feelings were just not okay to be shared. Being nice and liked was more important than being authentic or truthful.

I could see how this thread that being nice was more important than being authentic had woven itself through my entire life. In my twenties, I let the man I was dating pick the movies and went even when they weren't my first choice. I went with him to U.S.C. football games even though I'm not that big of a football fan. I went along with pretty much whatever he wanted to do. I never told him I was compromising myself. One day there was a play I really wanted to go see; I bought the tickets and I asked him if he would come with me. He said that he wasn't interested in going to the theater; he pronounced it with a British accent, "Theee-AH-TA" and said — "I'm not one of those Thee-Ah-Ta people." I was hurt. I wasn't a football person and I went to the games with him. I had never insisted on anything I wanted to do and had gone along with all the things he wanted to do and now he wouldn't do something with me that was important to me. Then I realized he never knew that I had made all those compromises. He thought we had the same interests and so if he didn't go to the theater with me, we still had a lot of things in common, right? Wrong! But it wasn't his fault. It was mine. He didn't know me at all.

No one, including me, really knew me because I kept twisting myself in different shapes to conform to what I thought others wanted, telling half truths, and hiding. Even though I thought I was being nice to people, what I became was a master self manipulator, and through that, a manipulator of others. I talked behind people's backs. I would offer things I couldn't deliver. I was flaky because I overcommitted myself rather than being honest. I didn't see it as lying at the time. It was woven so tightly into some part of my psyche that who I was at my core wasn't okay. No one should see what was inside me. I needed to hide it or die.

We are all trying not to be emotionally naked so that no one guesses how vulnerable and human we are. One day after I turned forty, I was having a conversation with my mother, and she asked how I was feeling about turning forty. I replied that I finally felt more comfortable in my own skin. To which my mom replied, "Carol. God wants you to wear clothes!" I shook my head as though I had misheard her and asked her what she had just said. She repeated: "God wants you to wear clothes. It is in the Bible!" "Where is it in the Bible, Mom?" "Modesty," my mom replied. I laughed quite hard after I hung up the phone. Imagining Art up in heaven saying to the angels, "Please make sure Carol Woodliff wears clothes!" I don't think God cares one way or another. If we go back to the story of Adam and Eve – God was quite fine with us naked. It was embarrassment at our humanness that caused us to be ashamed of our bodies and hide.

We clothe ourselves in stories that are half truths rather than risk being seen for the perfectly imperfect human beings we are. What I think we are all being asked to do is to be a different form of being naked – the nakedness of letting all our masks fall away – the nakedness of knowing that we are all at our heart scared of letting our humanness show.

Perhaps the biggest lie that so many of us have bought into is that our humanness is judged by God; that Art sits up in the sky saying, "I don't like the creation I made." I personally think God likes us naked, physically and emotionally. I don't think we are judged for being exactly what we were created to be – human! Although I'm not ready to run around without my clothes! I'm sure my mother is happy about that one.

As much as we say we don't like liars, we are very comfortable with being inauthentic. My clients quite regularly admit they are trying to morph themselves into something they think others want. They share with me something that is bothering them about a friend, family member or co-worker, and when I ask them if they've told the person what they are feeling, their response is, "I can't do that!" When I ask, "Why not?" the answer normally is something like, "I don't want to hurt their feelings" or, "It's not worth fighting over." "I'm afraid they'll leave or won't love me." I've been there! How many times have I stuffed down something that should have been discussed and said, "I can't tell them that!" when building a better, more authentic, relationship would come from sharing the hard truth?

On the other hand, not everything we think has to be shared. Like when my mom was trying to tell me that saying aloud my thoughts about someone's weight wasn't nice. I've certainly had times when people have shared things with me that make me want to scream, "TMI! Too much information!" There is this balance to be found of sharing our truths and being authentic and feeling like we have the right to share every thought that comes from our mind.

My biggest challenge is to not judge the darkness in myself or others. How easy it is to point the finger of blame at others for what we have within ourselves. When the politician is caught in a lie about his affair or the fundamentalist preacher is caught having a gay relationship, I have a tendency to be outraged and call them liars and hypocrites. It is easier to point the finger of judgment than to smile with compassion and say, "Ah, you are afraid too! You are lost. I've been there my friend. Sometimes we really screw up. We think we are hiding or taking the easy way out. I've been a hypocrite and a liar. I understand. I don't like what you are showing me about myself but I understand." How we put our parents, teachers, celebrities, and leaders on pedestals, and then feel let down when they are human. Instead of judging them when they are struggling, or showing us the shadow side of the human experience, it is healthier for us all to have some compassion.

It takes courage to be more transparent, more authentic and stop hiding. I think that is exactly what we are being called to do. It feels like spiritual skinny dipping — a little vulnerable and naked; scary, exhilarating and freeing at the same time. I know the world needs more of us to take the plunge and honor ourselves and others. The world doesn't need any more of our lies. The world doesn't need any more judgment. It needs us to be compassionate and forgiving when we think we need our stories to be loved. It needs us to see beneath the stories to the light we all may have forgotten is inside.

> **Think about your feelings about lying. When do you withhold your truth because it is easier or safer? When is it acceptable to keep your opinion to yourself? When do you find it easier to point the finger of blame? Are you ready to be more vulnerable or "naked" about your humanness?**

Chapter 12

WATCH WITH ME

No words are necessary. Simply be the witness. Be the light of love. Hold a hand, give a hug, be still and listen. Do not invalidate the pain. The pain is real but you are not your wounds and illnesses. You are so much more. Hold certain in each person's ability to find answers – to find the presence of the sacred within them. Hold the space for Spirit to work. Stand close by and know that this too is perfect. The Universe knows the right action.

Any action you take must begin with love. If you cannot move forward with love – do not move. Wait. Be still. Do not add to toxic energy by fighting it. Know that the only way out of the dark is by adding light, not adding more darkness. Heal your heart first and then send love, send light, send healing sunshine to help illuminate the way. If you cannot find love in the ugliness then you are the one missing the sacred – the oneness – in that situation. Judge not. The illusion that this is ugly, that this person is not connected, is a sign that you are not connected and need to find the heart of me within. All is one. What would love do? Practice rising above the darkness and judgment. Practice forgiving. Practice witnessing the sacred in all situations and all people.

~~~

"Being deeply loved by someone gives you strength, while loving someone deeply gives you courage." — Lao Tzu

~~~

In recent years, my most helpless moments have been witnessing my mother's deterioration. Each time I visited, I noticed her slipping a little bit more. Aging is a very interesting and often a seemingly cruel process. Watching a parent become someone that you don't recognize is sad and funny at the same time. My formerly strong, sturdy, proud "I can do anything" mother was now frail and curled up in a wheelchair. There were glimpses of her but more often than not I knew that Lucille, the mother I had growing up, would be appalled at some of her behavior. I do have an appreciation for how, as we age, we can say what we think and politeness be damned.

My sister told me of an incident when Mom was in rehab after her stroke and a woman was brought into the room in a full body cast. In full voice Mom yelled out, "What's her problem?" (This was definitely not the woman who said it wasn't nice to ask out loud why someone was fat!) Or the time, I sat with her in her assisted living home and an African American attendant came in to help her to the restroom. As the attendant left the room, Mom bellowed out, "Some of the coloreds are really nice!" I cringed and gently said, "Mom, they don't call them colored anymore." The attendant poked her head back in the room and winked at me! Bless her for not taking offense. Mom ignored me and issued her next set of orders: "Move my legs!" "Push me!" "Get me water!" The requests barked at me as though she was now the queen made me want to smile at her and ask, "What is the magic word?" as she used to do when I didn't say "please." But I understood that her stroke and the Parkinson's often made it difficult for her to speak. Short sentences worked better for her. I would often have to have her repeat herself again and again, because I didn't understand or she couldn't get a word out. The one word that came out loud and clear was "shit!" — her exclamation of frustration when things didn't go right. This was from a woman whose worst cuss words were "shoot" or "son of a sea cook." Yes, even when she was really angry, she rarely swore. *Shit* isn't exactly a hard-core swear word by today's standards, but if you knew her before the illness and aging, you'd have to laugh as it rang out loud and clear: "SHIT!"

Sometimes with medication, her body worked reasonably well and she could get around with a walker. Other days she was trapped needing to ask for help with the simplest tasks. "I hope this isn't genetic. I wouldn't want you to have to go through this." I would squeeze her hand. My voice would crack as I told her, "I wish you weren't going through this, Mom." It was heartbreaking to witness.

Even trapped in a body that was betraying her, I'd still get glimpses of the woman I grew up with. She'd be in her wheel chair, head slumped over to her chest and she'd ask me, "Have I eaten off all my lipstick?" I couldn't even see her lips as they were tucked down into her chest. I lifted her head gently and looked into her eyes. "Yes, Mom — your lipstick is gone!" "Put some on me," she would demand. I grabbed her lipstick and flashed to a moment a long time ago when I was a little girl and I'd stand next to her while she was getting ready and demand that she put lipstick on me. I looked at her lips — once full, now shriveled — and told her to "make like a fish so you don't end up looking like Joan Crawford." We laughed.

I put the lipstick on and handed her a hand mirror so she could look at herself. She looked confused for a second — like who is that old woman in the mirror? — then she put the mirror down, smiled and thanked me. The tears welled up in both our eyes. "A girl shouldn't go anywhere without her lipstick," I heard her say in my mind. Even as her body has betrayed her, the woman who stood in front of the mirror with me was in there somewhere.

She was aware that her body was deteriorating and it wasn't going to get better. That couldn't be easy for a woman who was always capable and self-sufficient and now had to rely on help for every part of her life. We could laugh or cry. Most days we laughed.

There were times when she would doze off in her wheelchair, and I would sit in her room with her with nothing to do but watch her sleep and other times when she couldn't move and whispered, "Help me!" She wanted me to roll the wheelchair back and forth or help her straighten her body in the chair. Sometimes she needed me to move her arms or legs or fix something in her apartment because she couldn't see well enough to see what was wrong with it. Part of me wished I could run. I didn't want to witness this. But another part knew that I just needed to be there. I needed to love her and allow her to be however she was that day.

The first days of a visit, I would recite monologues of things that were going on in my life and news from friends of mine that she knew from high school or college. By the second or third day of a visit, there wasn't much left to say. The only thing I could do was be with her for what little time I had to visit, and know that this could be the last time I saw her. As I sat listening to her labored breathing as she slept, a song that I used to sing at mass in grade school filtered back into my mind:

> Watch one hour with me
> Stay just a way by my side
> When my hallelujah days
> Streak into blues and grays
> Be my guide
> Stay awhile
> Watch with me[8]

It was almost as though an angel was singing inside my head so that I would remember what was important. There is the time we measure by calendars and clocks and then there is God's time or the time of the Universe. There are moments when time stands still because we are fully present. When we are just there for one another—not to do anything, but just be there. My job wasn't to fix things for her. It was to watch for an hour—to witness with love.

It sounds simple but it wasn't. It wasn't pleasant or happy. I wanted to make it better but I couldn't. All I could do was to be present in that moment. With my mom that meant patiently sitting and pushing her wheelchair back and forth, if that was the best we could do that day, or taking her

---

[8] Watch With Me by Joe Wise ©1972 /Gia Publications Inc., used by permission.

for a stroll around her assisted-living home by pushing her chair; or on a really lucky day sitting with her in the swing on the front porch of the home reminiscing about the porch swing on my grandparents' front porch—then sitting and rocking silently together. No agenda—no rushing off to do something. Just being. Little did I know when I would bitch to my friends about "my difficult mother" how much I would miss her when she was no longer "my difficult mother."

As I said earlier, I can't remember a time in my childhood or early adulthood when she actually said the words, "I love you." I knew she did, but she rarely, if ever, said it. She showed it by staying up all night sewing those dresses—not in words. A couple of years ago, after her first stroke, I decided that every time I spoke to her I would tell her I loved her. I knew that each phone conversation or visit could be our last so I made the commitment to make sure each time she heard me say, "I love you." In the beginning it was rocky. I'd say, "I love you, Mom" and she'd either snort or say, "I know." Whether she ever said it back didn't matter. I was going to give her the gift with no expectation in return. Then one day it happened. I was ending a phone conversation and I said, "I love you, Mom" and she said it back, "I love you, too!" I cried. After that each phone conversation ended with me saying, "I love you" and her replying, "I love you, too!" Sometimes she'd even beat me to it and say it first. I would hang up the phone knowing that could be the last time I'd hear her voice and I was glad we'd gotten to this place, where no words were left unspoken.

One visit when I was leaving to go to California, I stopped by my mom's room to say goodbye. She had had several bad days during my visit but this day was a good day. We talked for about a half hour and when I got up to leave, she got up and walked me with her walker out to the end of her hallway. She put her arms out and I fell into the first standing body-to-body hug I'd had from her in five years. She looked at me and said without prompting, "I love you—thanks for coming!" I got to hug back hard and say, "I love you. Thanks for being my mom!" I walked to my rental car with tears streaming down my face and gave thanks. No matter when the end came, I'd always have that perfect moment to remember. And I'd be happy that I committed to sitting with her even when part of me wanted to be somewhere else and didn't know what to do—that I created a loving space where we could just be.

I remember this when I'm faced with other difficult situations. Sometimes it is as simple and as difficult as watching for an hour without judgment, witnessing and being love. Many times that is all we can do.

What are you being asked to witness? Is it hard for you to be with someone when you know that you can't fix their situation? When have you found that presence is more important than any words you might say?

CHAPTER 13

THE GIFTS IN THE TRIGGERS

You got triggered. You are frustrated and upset. The world is not the way you think it is supposed to be and you find yourself not living at your highest. Relax! Here is your opportunity. Look at the wounds of the past. Feel the feeling. Look at what you have been hiding and the story you have been telling. You cannot move to love without acknowledging what is. If you are hurt and angry, you cannot pretend that you are not. If you are scared and feeling vulnerable, like you will never get it, pretending that all is well without looking at those feelings honestly will not help you grow.

Every person here is your teacher. Bless those who cause strong emotions and make you want to fight or run away. They show you your darkness and your hidden wounds. They are like you. There is no comparison, no competition, no better or worse than. Any evil you perceive in the world cannot be managed with hate or drama. You, however, have the perfect opportunity to be triggered and be truthful with yourself and work your way back to love.

These moments are gifts wrapped in paper you think ugly. But before you throw them out as worthless, before you run away, look those beautiful feelings in the face. Those feelings are your latest opportunity to grow. See where you are caught up in a story and ask for help to move to your highest place. The Universe is designed to lead you to your highest potential — if you don't turn away from its triggers and gifts. Under the ugly wrappings and pain, love is always there. If you were triggered today, your consciousness is ready to see the light — see the next level of the journey.

A trigger is an invitation to move closer to me. Recognize that every moment of discomfort is a blessing. It cannot be attacked. It must be surrounded with love. It is asking you to move beyond, to look to the highest you can imagine and go there. Take a step in that direction. Exhale and let go of the breath. Practice dying to the story. Look for the gift. Rise up.

It matters not whether it takes you minutes or hours or years to see the gift. Triggers are your homework. Like the homework assignments or not, work through them when you are ready and remember the only answer is love. If you see the same events coming round and round again, you have another level of love to find. It is perfect, you are never left behind.

Whatever you are experiencing right now is the doorway into the next level of your transformation. It is only in stepping into what you perceive as a challenge with love that you can be transformed. See with new eyes, feel with new heart, think with the mind of God, speak with lips of love, and act for the best of all.

~~~

"[E]verything in life has purpose. There are no mistakes, no coincidences, all events are blessings given to us to learn from." —Elisabeth Kübler-Ross

~~~

I had hoped that this connection with my Sacred Voice would mean I wouldn't have those embarrassing "not spiritual" moments. But I have come to realize that all the times I've labeled myself as not good enough, or had a moment when I've been rather embarrassed at my lack of being a spiritual presence in the world, have actually been some of my greatest teachers. They show me where the next doorway is for me to walk through in my own personal growth. They show me when I'm not living in alignment with my sacredness and I'm letting those smaller voices take control.

One Friday in 2009, I was returning home at one in the morning after a late shift at the law firm. I drove down the alley toward my driveway parking area that I share with my neighbors, and I noticed a rather large SUV parked diagonally across the whole space—taking up both my neighbor's and my spot. I remembered that my neighbors had told me that they were going to be out of town that weekend and were having a woman from a new pet/house sitting service stay at the house while they were gone. I was tired after a very long day and it was shocking how quickly my anger and blood pressure rose as these thoughts raced through my mind: "You've got to be f'ing kidding me! How dare the pet sitter park in my spot? I hate people with SUVs who think they own the road." First I honked my horn. Then I put the hazard lights on, left my car in the middle of the alley and marched straight up to the house. I pounded on the door. No one answered. I grabbed my phone, dialed their number and let the phone ring until the voice mail picked up. I knew the pet sitter couldn't access the voice mail, so I dialed and hung up several times and then I banged on the door again.

Somewhere in the midst of this, I became aware that my behavior was quite irrational. If I were staying in a strange house and someone started banging on the door after one in the morning, I'm pretty sure I wouldn't answer either! I knew that the pet sitter was probably just unaware that two cars parked in that area. I doubted she pulled up and said, "I think I'll really tick off Carol. I know what I'll do. I'll park in her space!" I knew I was acting ridiculously but a voice inside kept repeating, "Damn it! I want my space *now!*"

A part of me was watching the arguments between rational Carol and irrational Carol. It was rather like a tennis match — watching both sides of my brain volley back and forth. Swinging from the kind, "She didn't mean it," to the outraged and vengeful, "That witch! How dare she?" From, "Is there really a problem? Grab a couple of bucks and go buy a nightly parking permit so you can park on the street without getting a ticket!" to, "You can't just let people take advantage of you. I'm not spending money when I have a space."

The rational part stepped in to negotiate, "She's not answering the door. You are not going to get your space tonight. The sooner you accept that fact and park the car on the street, the sooner you can go to bed. Put a note on her car so she knows not to do it again — just in case she is gone before you get up in the morning." "Deal!" my grumpy self agreed. I moved my car to the street deciding to risk the ticket rather than driving to the vending machine at City Hall to get the overnight permit. I went in the house, jotted off a terse note, and went back outside to tuck it on her windshield. Still fuming, I let the wiper drop back with a loud slap on the windshield and allowed the back gate to slam on the way into my house. Rational voice stepped in "What are you, two years old? Stop it. Stop having a tantrum. Why are you being so territorial? You might as well go pee on her car to mark your turf!" I started to giggle at that mental picture. My anger dissipated as I laughed

When I woke up the next day, the SUV was gone. I did some errands and came home. Later that evening I went out to my car to go somewhere and on my car was a note from the pet sitter. "I'm so, so sorry. It won't happen again." As I read her note I was embarrassed at how I had overreacted. Thank goodness there was a more rational part of me that kept stepping forward saying, "Let it go."

As I reflected on this incident a few days later, I was amazed at how that parking space became my West Bank or Gaza Strip in that moment. "That's my territory and I'll fight you for it!" (I'm very clear that the situation on the West Bank or Gaza is much more complicated than my parking space upset.) I was able to hold my reactions to a little door banging, phone calling and a terse note but it wasn't the "me" I wanted to be. My anger was so out of proportion to the event. Why was I so triggered? What caused me to be so protective of my turf? Why couldn't I let it go the moment I drove up and then ask her not to do it again in the morning? In the time I spent raging, I could have been to city hall and back with the permit. If you'd asked me if I would pay the $2 cost for an overnight street parking to avoid feeling rage, I normally would have said yes, but that night my answer was no. I was hooked and even though part of me knew it was irrational to feel that way, I couldn't unhook myself. I had lost my intelligence and reason and found myself wondering, "What happened? How did I get here?"

I know it is more helpful to believe that the things that happen to me are here to teach me something rather than holding onto the idea that everything is out to get me. So what was the gift in the trigger of the parking spot incident? What was the part of me that I wasn't seeing? I go back to what was happening at the time. I'd been working a lot and had just finished a seventeen-hour day. I was worried about my mother's care expenses. She had run out of money and I wasn't making enough to chip in much for her care. I was trying to work extra hours at the law firm and up my marketing efforts for the business. I was so busy getting things done. Everything caught up with me. I was tired and cranky. What did I need? Not so much a parking space as I needed to stop expecting myself to be superwoman. I was the one taking advantage of myself. It wasn't about where the car was parked. It was about where I allowed other people to be entitled to take care of their needs, but I didn't take care of my own. I realized that the SUV was a big symbol for me of other people's entitlement. I was angry because I wasn't taking up space in my own life. It took me a few days to see it.

Trigger moments are the opportunity to notice the seeds of disconnection and disharmony we feel within, the dark places or shadow parts we would rather not own. They are awakenings that allow us to choose to stay with the same old beliefs and behaviors that brought us to that moment or to let go of past conditioning and stories. Each moment in which we let go of old beliefs is an exercise in trust. It is allowing spirit to work. And it is indeed an opportunity to practice letting part of ourselves die—old ideas of how things have to be done or how they should be. We experience little deaths—a relationship ends, we lose a job, a parking spot is taken. These are opportunities to notice what we are holding onto that keeps us from connecting with our authentic loving self.

Every time we are frustrated or triggered it is an invitation to grow our hearts. Each trigger is a gift that asks us to move closer to our true sacred self. It is unrealistic to imagine that we will never have a strong reaction to something, that we will never get triggered again. It is healthier to see the trigger as an invitation to look deeper. These triggers are doorways of understanding and opportunities for growth.

> **Can you look back at times you were triggered and now see what the event was trying to teach you? What did you need to see and accept in yourself? What did you need to process, release or heal? How did the trigger invite you to move closer to your spirit? What was the gift?**

CHAPTER 14

SEE ALL WITH LOVE

Love is always there. You are the one who forgets. Soften and open your heart. Take a breath and feel it flow through you. See the connection in all things. Love flows through every particle of this universe. You are all one. You spend much time looking at your own and other people's deficiencies and failings and very little time being love. Love those who call you names, because you have spoken against others. Love those who cheat you, because you also have been miserly. See those who can't see and act from love — the murderer, the terrorist, the thief, the liar — with eyes of love, because they have lost their way. You have lost yours, too.

You cannot bring light if you choose that only certain people and events deserve love. Cultivate compassion. Everyone, absolutely everyone, deserves love because they are part of your world. See all with love. You do not hurt them when you withhold your love. You hurt yourself.

Go inward first. What you do not recognize or see in yourself you will always see in the world. What you love and accept within yourself will allow you to love and accept in the world. Love your light and have compassion for your darkness. Then go out in the world and love the light and darkness there. Honor the capacity of darkness in the world and shine your light upon it.

Practice loving your world as it is today. Practice being me in the moments that frustrate you. Practice being me when you are sad, scared and angry. Practice being me with those you disagree with. Practice being me when it is dark. Remember the light is always there. The Divine is there when you are willing to honor and align with your highest, not judge. Grow compassion in your heart so big that it envelops the world. What can you do to make heaven in your corner of the world today? Right now with your worries, how can you love? What can you do right now, in this moment to open your heart to yourself and your world? What can you do today to make sacred every encounter you have? I don't expect you to be perfect. I expect you to practice remembering the perfection that exists with love.

~~~

"Perhaps everything terrible is in its deepest being something helpless that wants help from us."

— Rainer Maria Rilke

~~~

Seeing all with love sounds good but can we admit how incredibly hard it can be to actually put that into practice? When this lesson came through, my mind immediately flashed back to someone I didn't think I could ever love. In 1975, when I was in the eighth grade, a classmate of mine was abducted from his morning paper route and taken to a cabin where he was molested, tortured and murdered. He was fifteen. It was a crime that shook my hometown. My parents protected me from the details of the crime, and, fortunately, at fourteen, I was sheltered enough not to understand exactly how brutal it was. But his murder has stayed with me for the rest of my life.

He was the first person my age that I knew who had died. Initially, I decided I didn't want to go to the funeral. Funerals were creepy and he wasn't a close friend of mine. But when the day of the funeral came, I knew I had to go. I knew I needed to tell him that I cared what happened to him. He was a kind young man, who loved to laugh, but he was also the kid that got made fun of by some of the students in class. He wasn't one of the smartest boys, the most athletic or the most handsome, but there was a sweetness there that we didn't acknowledge until it was too late. His death made me realize that while I wasn't one of the people making fun of him, I also wasn't one of the people standing up for him. I saw others tease him and did nothing. I don't know whether I was really able to articulate this to myself at fourteen, but in the coming years, I realized that sometimes you don't get another chance to say what you should have said or do what you had an impulse to do. You might not get another chance to be kind to someone.

His murderer was sentenced to 150 years in prison, but due to the law he was sentenced under at the time, he is now eligible for a parole hearing each year. My classmate's family has had to withstand at least 17 parole hearings and testify or send impact statements to make sure this man is not back on the street again. To date, there has not been one vote cast in favor of parole.

I hesitated in writing about this event. I wouldn't want to add to his family's pain. But when I read the message "love murderers," that classmate's face flashed into my mind. His murder is imprinted in my fourteen-year-old psyche. My mind spins when I contemplate the cold-blooded reality of his death and the idea of loving the man who caused it. I hear the teaching of Jesus, "Love your enemies and pray for those who persecute you," and part of me knows I am supposed to step up and at least try to love him. Another part says absolutely not! How could I love a child molester and murderer? How could I love a terrorist? How could I love and forgive them when they caused so much pain? These are the questions that make my head and heart hurt. I don't know how.

This is deep work. Work that I feel very inept at. My mind turns back to Jesus, arrested and sentenced to death — tortured and paraded through the streets of town so people could mock and humiliate him. And as he died, what did he say? "Father forgive them for they know not what they do!" Not: "I hate you bastards for what you've done!" Not: "I hope you burn in hell!" Not: "I'll get you for this!" But "Forgive them because they don't know what they are doing." When I contemplate that prayer made by Jesus while suffering a terrible death, I can truly see how loving the Christ Consciousness is. In his deepest pain, his thoughts were on love and forgiveness. I know we are called to follow that example. I am supposed to remember that when people don't act out of love, it is because they have lost their way. I am called to remember that deep inside that person there is a connection to spirit that has been obscured by the darkness of the action they have taken, and I am supposed to love the spirit deep inside. I would prefer to judge the action and condemn the person. But a higher part of me says, "You can do better!" I'm not sure that I can, or even want to do that. The closest I can come is to love who they were as babies when they came into the world before something went wrong. Loving these people when their actions are heinous feels so far from where I am; it feels impossible.

I was talking about this with a friend, and she automatically said, "Carol. You are being too hard on yourself. You aren't Jesus. It's okay to not love that man." Part of me wanted to breathe a sigh of relief and let myself off the hook, but I couldn't. Deep inside there is sacredness in learning to love what feels unlovable. But loving that murderer seems like graduate school loving and I'm not there yet. It is pretty easy to mouth, "See all with love"; it is so much harder to actually live by that edict. Life gives me endless opportunities every day to practice, opportunities woven into everyday moments and I often find that it isn't so easy or automatic to see with love.

- I get upset with the woman who is talking loudly on her cell phone in the grocery store, sharing far too much very personal information. *No I don't want to know about your date last night and how good he was in bed. Shut Up!!* I say to myself as I throw dirty looks her way. Wrapped up in her conversation she is oblivious to my judgment of her.

- I turn on the news or browse the Internet and see lots of people spouting opinions laced with hate in contentious debates about national policy. My mind starts a running commentary as I disagree: *What idiots! How can they say that? Why are there so many mean, nasty people in the world?*

- Outraged at the man in the blue pickup truck who cuts me off on the narrow, winding Pasadena freeway that leads into my town, I hear myself swearing at him and shaking my head feeling justified in my anger.

- I listen to someone at work whine about a co-worker when I know the person is never going to have a conversation with that person to their face. And yet I participate in the gossip or complaint rather than walking away, standing up for that person or moving the conversation toward finding a solution.

None of these seem that awful but they certainly aren't loving actions; and if I can't be loving in these petty moments, how am I going to do it with the big stuff? I hear, *I don't expect you to be perfect, I just expect you to practice. When you become aware of being less than loving, choose again. It is possible. And that includes loving yourself, too!* I know it is. I did it with the man in the blue pickup truck. In the middle of my tirade about stupid drivers, I was able to catch myself and say, "It isn't like you have never done a stupid thing while driving, Carol. You don't know what is on his mind!" I sent prayers after my curses.

This whole idea of doing everything with love means that I can't run on autopilot. I need to be awake. Am I moving toward hate or love? Am I going to live from my fear or my higher self? Am I going to try to justify why it is okay for me to hate? If the root of all harm is the absence of love, I cannot throw hate at the absence of love and expect that to make the world a better place. This is the calling of the sacred: to choose to see love even in the most difficult circumstances.

I set this chapter aside for several months. I didn't have an ending. And then I realized it all came down to the Golden Rule, "Do unto others as you would have them do unto you." If I descended far into darkness, would I want condemnation or would I want people praying for me? It isn't a difficult question to answer. Of course, I'd want people praying and hoping that I found the light again. More condemnation and hurt wouldn't help me. I would need love. My mind wants to come up with all sorts of reasons why I don't have to love "those people," but my spirit says hate only creates more hate.

So I took a deep breath and I visualized my heart connecting with the most loving sacred heart of the Universe—"God, the Universe, Source—whoever or whatever you are—help me see this with your eyes. Help me see all situations in my life and in my world with love. I pray for all the people whom I have judged, including myself. I pray for all the people whom I have called evil, and I pray for those that they hurt with their actions. Through the healing power of love, help us all find our way to connection with our highest selves. Help me find my light. Help me see those who have lost their way in love. Help me see myself as love. Help me be love." And that prayer felt really good. It doesn't mean to me that there shouldn't be consequences for unacceptable behavior in society; it means the consequences should be conceived in love, not revenge.

The only answer I have for myself right now is to ask Spirit for help. When I see myself being judgmental and I know my heart is closed to loving someone who has done something on the scale of somewhere between the annoying and the outright horrific, I need to ask that highest source of love to open both our hearts. When I can't see or be love, I can ask for help—even for a murderer. And perhaps one day, I will find that I am ready to say I can love that man. But for today, I am willing to ask for Spirit's help to expand my capacity for love for the woman in the grocery store, the man in the pickup truck, for my co-workers, family and friends, for those who are so hard to love because they have done the unthinkable, and for myself as I do the best I can today. The most important growth I can achieve is to expand my ability to love what I feel at this moment is unlovable in me and others. I know my heart still has lots of room to grow in its capacity for love. How can I shift a little closer to seeing all with love?

> **Where is it a stretch to love someone? Can you ask God/the Universe to help you shift a little closer to love, to help you see things differently?**

CHAPTER 15

BLESSED ENDINGS

The beginnings and endings are just pauses where you see what is true. Your joy and your sadness soften and open you. There is no separation. The curtain is pulled back and your heart connects if you let it. You are aware of your part in the oneness. In those moments you remember. You are so present that time stops. You break open. The cracks let the light in. There is beauty in those moments and yet you fear them most. You live your life pretending that these moments don't exist. You hope somehow you will escape the inevitable. You hope that if you ignore the fact that this life is fragile and your time here is temporary, you will cheat death for yourself and all those you love.

You are not separate. You are not alone. No one leaves you. They and you are part of the whole. There is no beginning or ending, just opportunities to go deeper. Only in fully living each birth and death do you have capacity to remind yourself of who you are: beautiful soul, beautiful spirit, coming in and out of a body.

Dancing the dance of life — whirling, enjoying, laughing, crying and then returning to source after the grand adventure. Bringing back to spirit the wonderful energy of how you — this beautiful soul — contributed to the experience that is life.

Gather the threads of connection and weave them into a new cloth. Open yourself to the song in your heart. Let it play in the world. Hear your song answered back reverberating throughout the universe. What you need will appear. It is already there. When your heart changes you will see the connections, the messages, the love that vibrates through every molecule of the universe. When you see with eyes of insight so that your physical eyes will see that everything here is a miracle and there is nothing, NOTHING that is not.

~~~

"Ever has it been that love knows not its own depth until the hour of separation."
—Kahlil Gibran

~~~

The Friday before Memorial Day, 2010, I got a message from my sister that Mom was being taken to the hospital with pneumonia. Over the last eight years Mom had been in and out of the hospital several times. I was concerned but not alarmed. I told my sister to keep me posted on what the doctors said and began to prepare to make the journey back to Illinois, if it was necessary. I waited it out over the weekend and Mom seemed to be doing a bit better. But by the following Thursday, I got the call that Mom wasn't responding to the three different antibiotics they had given her. My sister Luanne and I agreed it was time to move her to hospice care and let her go. My sister kept telling me, "I don't know what to tell you to do. She is dying but I don't know how long she has." I hung up the phone and got very quiet and listened. The Voice said, "*Go Monday!*" I went to the Internet and found a round-trip ticket for a flight leaving Monday for $267 with a connection in Minneapolis. All the direct flights to Chicago were over $700. I knew Monday was the day I was supposed to fly. I stood at my kitchen sink as I did dishes Friday night and imagined a light traveling from my heart all the way to my mother in her hospital bed. I sent love and told her that I would be there on Monday evening but that if she needed to go before then, I would understand. As the daughter that was out of town I knew each time I saw my mom in these last years, it could be my last visit. Everything had been said. I wanted to be there if I could be but I knew that it might not happen.

Monday afternoon, I called my sister to check in as I drove from the airport. Mom had been moved back to the nursing home for her final days. I headed directly there and entered her room. Lying in the bed with an oxygen tube in her nose was my mother — unconscious, frail, weighing less than 120 pounds. (This was painfully thin for her. I don't remember her ever weighing less than 150 in my childhood and adult life.) I kissed her forehead and took her hand, "Momma, it's Carol, I'm here. I love you. You waited for me, didn't you?" She gently squeezed my hand back but didn't open her eyes. The nursing home staff handed me a mask because of the various strains of antibiotic-resistant bacteria in Mom's lungs. The hospice nurse looked at me and said, "You can choose to wear it or not. Love will protect you." I wasn't sure whether those two sentences were related or not. Was she talking about the mask or that love would help me as I sat vigil and became the midwife of my mother's transition to the other side?

When Mom first entered the hospital, I asked family and friends to pray for her healing. Then when it became apparent that it was her time, I asked for prayers that angels and guides would meet her to help her make her journey with ease and grace. I felt surrounded by the energy of those prayers and strengthened by love.

I sat with her telling her she had done a good job; that I loved her for everything that she had done for me, and that I would be okay. I thought of all of her imperfections that I focused on as a child and as a young adult with the light of spirit and love. I realized that I had often thought people saw their loved ones with rose-colored glasses when they died. But now I realized that in these moments, the most pure love allows all of our filters of judgment to fall away. I told her that if it was time for her to go, we understood and it was okay. I stroked her hair which was a mess after lying in bed for over a week. Mom always had her hair done every week. She would be appalled. I brushed her hair gently.

Luanne, who had carried the burden of so much of Mom's care, came by. I could see the stress of the last weeks in her eyes and for a moment felt guilt that I hadn't been here sooner. My sister had done so much heavy lifting over the last eight years, juggling her job, family and looking after Mom. I could be the one to sit bedside and hold vigil while my sister came and went and took care of the rest of her life. I was surprised at how certain I was that I could be the witness. If you had asked me years ago, I would have said, I don't want to be there when a loved one passes. Now I knew it was one of my greatest gifts.

As a hypnotherapist, I am trained in imagery for the ill and dying. I have studied Reiki and other energy techniques.

As I sat with Mom, talking with her, I began to use all the techniques that I had been trained in. I started at her feet, massaging gently and moving up her body; I paid special attention to each chakra area — imagining and intending that I was releasing any energy that would keep her stuck in her body. As I gently touched her she settled and relaxed into a more restful sleep.

The radio was on near her bedside; I jokingly told her that I couldn't find a Brewer's game for her to listen to as I tuned the station to an easy listening station that seemed to have gentle music. Mom was a passionate sports fan for her teams. My childhood was spent with Mom having more than one radio tuned to college or pro football, baseball, basketball games — multiple games at one time. I rebelled against sports to differentiate myself from her. Now here I was hoping to find a game on the radio for her. Instead it was as though the program director was orchestrating our goodbye: "Because You Loved Me" sung by Celine Dion (by Diane Warren) was followed by "Have I Told You Lately" sung by Rod Stewart (by Van Morrison) followed by "Let It Be" performed by The Beatles (by John Lennon and Paul McCartney). Tears streamed down my face as I listened to the lyrics of each song and sang the words to my mom. And the songs continued. I sang to her. I cried and couldn't sing. I placed my hand on her heart and my other hand on mine and let the love flow through me to her and all the while I imagined her being released from the body that was now a shell of whom she had been. The radio began the news at the top of the hour. I sang church songs — "Amazing Grace", and "Be Not Afraid" — half singing, half talking the lyrics to her as the tears streamed down my face.

The staff of the home came in and out to check on Mom, brought her medication to help her stay comfortable and turned her every couple of hours. It was hard to watch her grimace as they moved her to avoid bed sores. I knew they were doing the best for her but part of me thought, why disturb her? She had such limited time.

Each time I needed a short break for lunch or the restroom, I kissed her and told her where I was going and gave her my blessing that if it was time to go while I was gone it was okay.

Visitors stopped by. The hairdresser who did Mom's hair every week came by and cried, "She was fine a week ago when I did her hair!" She told me how much she enjoyed my mother and what a great woman she was. We cried together. She saw the picture of the sacred heart sitting by mom's bedside and asked, "Are you Catholic? I have a prayer card I want to get for you—it is a rosary novena that can be said for the dying." I don't think I had said a rosary since my father's wake twenty-three years before. But I took the prayer card she gave me and knew I was supposed to say the rosary for Mom. It was her prayer. My voice cracked at the first Hail Mary, which ends with "Holy Mary Mother of God, pray for us sinners now and at the hour of our death, amen." I didn't think Mom was much of a sinner. As my father said years ago, she was a good woman; but I knew the prayer would bring her comfort. I said it for her and then added my own. "Carry her on angel wings home to the light and love that is the source of all. Allow her to reunite with my father and her family who passed before her. Let there be peace and beauty there."

More people stopped by who had cared for my mom in her last years. "She was such an amazing lady," "so appreciative of our help." The hospice workers were so kind, offering to get me sodas or food, giving me phone numbers to call if I wanted to talk. They were all angels of support.

Late in the evening on Tuesday, I heard Mom's voice in my head saying, "For heaven's sake go home and get some sleep. You don't need to sit up all night." I smiled. It certainly sounded like her. Once again I kissed her goodbye and promised I'd be back in the morning. "If it is easier for you to leave tonight when I'm not here, it's okay, Mom. I love you!" I said as I walked out the door. Wednesday morning I walked back into her room. Her skin was greyer. She looked even smaller. I knew that today would be the day. I continued with my bedside monologues and songs. I kept a cool cloth on her forehead because she was running a fever. I wiped her mouth with citrus flavored swabs and small sponges dipped in water to ease her dry mouth. I smiled as her eyebrows rose with a look of delight from the citrus flavor. She was pretty much unresponsive and I took comfort in doing something small that gave her a little pleasure or comfort. "You did a good job, Mom. It is okay to go. You've got a whole welcoming committee waiting for you. Go dance with Dad. We love you but it is time for you to leave this body that isn't working so well anymore and fly free." I thought perhaps she was holding on for us so I whispered in her ear. "Mom, I know you want to stay and help us but your body won't let you do that here. I know you will be so much more powerful on the other side. It's okay to let this body go. I'm looking forward to seeing what miracles you can perform from the other side." I'd run out of things to say and I'd just go back to stroking her arm or hair. I'd lay my hand on her chest and imagine healing, soothing energy entering her heart. Things were simple. I was holding vigil for her. There was nothing really for me to do except love and witness.

It was a challenging day. The nursing home was doing some upgrading construction and there was lots of noise in the hallway. A construction worker stuck his head in the room to ask me if he could replace the closet door in the room. I said, "Not today. You can do it tomorrow." I knew as I looked back at Mom on the bed, the room would be empty tomorrow. Mom was no longer in her body. I could feel it. The body was still breathing but Mom's essence was in the room and I felt it above me. It actually came and went several times that day as though she was practicing crossing over.

Luanne came by in the late afternoon and told me that her daughter, Rachel wanted to stop by but that Rachel's son, Sean, my mother's only great grandchild, couldn't come in the room because he was too young to be exposed to the bacteria that had caused Mom's illness. As we talked, Mom's breathing started to change. It was like someone with sleep apnea. She'd breathe out and there'd be a long pause. Then she'd breathe in again. It was much more peaceful than what I thought a death rattle would sound like.

My sister counted the pauses in between Mom's breaths. As a nurse, Luanne knew that we were approaching the end and that any out breath could be Mom's last. This went on for quite a while. Luanne and I were talking over the bed and we noticed that Mom hadn't taken a breath back in. We hadn't been counting. Luanne took Mom's pulse. She was gone. It was peaceful. I knew that she would have heard us chatting and thought, "They are going to be okay. My job is done here. And if I can't have one last meeting with my great grandson I'm out of here!" Mom was always concerned that we two girls stay close, and with eight years' difference in age and 1700 miles between us this wasn't always easy. "You are the only sisters you are going to have. It's important to love each other," she'd say. With her two daughters by her side chatting, Mom had released her last breath. I knew that she was now with my father and so many of her family members that had gone before her. I kissed her forehead one last time and said, "I love you, Mommy, go be at peace." The nursing home staff told us to stay as long as we wanted; my sister and I looked at each other and knew Mom was no longer in the room. We hugged and left in our separate cars, to begin the process of notifying relatives.

The Saturday of my mother's funeral was a gray day with thunder showers threatening. My sister and I planned a beautiful and simple funeral service at the church that she helped found and where she spent those years volunteering. The day before, my sister and I had joked with the parish priest, Father Joel, about how Mom always used to say she was ironing her way to heaven as she toiled with the linen altar cloths as part of her altar lady duties. Our home did not have air conditioning and on those Midwestern humid summer days, ironing the many yards long of fabric that had to be kept damp, with the steam rising off the cloth as she pressed, must have indeed felt like purgatory. Father Joel had never met my mother and we were sharing stories with him of her love of this church and community so that he would know the woman he was helping to bury.

We had decided to forgo an evening visitation the night before and have a viewing in the parish hall at the church immediately before the funeral. Relatives would be traveling from Minnesota and Wisconsin. I prayed that the predicted thunderstorms would hold off so that everyone would have a safe journey and that we could do the graveside service at the cemetery without danger.

Mom's family has a tradition of having a family reunion picnic in Prairie du Chien, Wisconsin, on the first Sunday in August each year. These family gatherings were the highlight of my summers as a child. The extended family of great aunts and uncles and their families made for a large gathering, many times of over 150 people. Mom loved those gatherings and the time with "the boys," as my mom called her brothers. Years passed, and Mom's generation moved from being the people that put on the picnic to the elder heads of the family that were helped to the picnic tables and told to sit and rest. I distinctly remember the moment when I looked around one of these picnics and realized that I had become one of the ladies that put the food on the table as opposed to one of the kids or helpers.

As years went by, the first of Mom's brothers passed away and others were too infirm to make it. It wasn't the same without my whole group of uncles, teasing, joking and playing cards, and telling the kids to stay out of the cooler with the beer or "adult beverages" as we called them as children. Mom had her stroke in 2002. Between the stroke and her Parkinson's, her mobility wasn't good enough for a journey to a picnic three and a half hours away. Her spirit so wanted to make it, but her body just wasn't capable. It hurt so much when she'd say she wanted to go to the picnic and I knew we couldn't make it happen for her.

So here at the church, our extended family was gathering to honor her life and I thought how pleased she'd be to see us together. She loved this big, loud and teasing family of hers. With each cousin I hugged, I knew Mom would be pleased that so many had traveled to say goodbye.

I walked to the area of the room where Mom's body was available to pay last respects — in a corner of the room with a screen creating some privacy, with two tall windows in the corner on each side. I looked out one of the windows and noticed there were two ducks, a female and a mallard. There is no pond anywhere near the church. The river is over a mile away. But there they were right outside looking in at me and the family gathering. I got goose bumps and felt comfort in their presence.

When I was little, my mom, dad, sister and I would often go feed the ducks at the Sinissippi Gardens pond in the summer. I remember my dad telling me that ducks, like people, mate for life. Those two ducks looked like a happy couple and seemed intent on checking out the goings on in that parish hall. Could it be that the spirits of my mom and dad were using the ducks to tell me it was okay? I had spent the two days prior to my mother's death telling her that it was okay to go and that my father was waiting for her. "Fly free!" I kept telling her. As I looked out the window, it was as if my mom and dad were checking in on the family gathering that my mom would have so loved. Later that night back at my sister's house, I did a little research on the Internet on the Native American wisdom about ducks and found one site that said ducks bring the message of family connections, emotional healing, and calming influences.[9] The message was perfect for someone at a funeral. Several days later I wrote on my blog about the two ducks at the funeral. Later that day, I received an email from a friend from Facebook who asked if I minded if she shared something with me. She said she was a medium and had a message for me. She said, "You already know this, but the ducks are from your parents who wanted you to know that they were sad they had to leave you but that you aren't alone." She shared the name and variations of lyrics from the Cole Porter "I Get a Kick Out of You." I got chills and began to cry as I read the email because Cole Porter was definitely their music.

A couple of days after my mom passed, I received a "Today I Believe God Wants You to Know" email from Neale Donald Walsch that ended with the phrase, "sadness cleanses the heart." It described exactly how I felt. I had felt the richness of sorrow and let it flow through me, and tapped into a deep well of love inside. My heart was so open. The sadness came from the loss of the "this world" relationship with my mother, but I also knew it was best for her to move on. I realized in these moments that when we don't give ourselves permission to feel sad over losing something, we diminish our capacity to love. We can be very sad and still not be unhappy. Being in that state and letting the loss flow through me without fighting it was one of the richest, most beautiful experiences of my life.

When my father passed away, I was twenty-six. I didn't have that much experience in loss. I thought it would break me. What surprised me was that instead of breaking from the

---

[9] http://healing.about.com/od/animaltotems/ig/Animal-Totems-Photo-Gallery/Duck.htm

loss of my father, I found myself so much more compassionate and open to other people's suffering. My heart was more available to others. And knowing that the sadness of my father's loss hadn't broken me made me more open to the pain and sadness I felt in my mother's passing.

There are sacred moments when the curtain between the spirit world and our human world is pulled back. I've had the blessing of being with my friend Judy when she gave birth to her daughter, Ellin, and at Mom's bedside as she passed. To date these are the most beautiful, profound moments of my life. Before each experience I was terrified that I wouldn't know what to do or say—that I wouldn't be enough. Now I know what I was most afraid of was an illusion. The beginnings and endings of life remind us of who we really are and distill life into its most important essence. We are love and we enter a body to express it. Our body is not who we are because before there is life and after there is life, there is still perfect love. In watching Ellin come into the world all new and innocent, I could see the beauty of the newness of life—my heart was full of love and hope. In the days that my mother was transitioning back to spirit, I could feel her essence in the room but not in that body, and I knew that she was going to be there beyond the time that her body would allow. I knew a deep unconditional love for her, my sister and myself and the world. It was beautiful, rich, sad, joyful and amazing. And I'm more connected to spirit because of those experiences. Love really is all that we are, and it is enough.

Have you had an experience where sadness cleansed your heart? Have you had an intense spirit experience of a loved

one's passing? Did it crack you open or shut you down?

CHAPTER 16

SIGNS & SYNCHRONICITIES

Signs are all around — small nods of yes, subtle encouragements placed to keep you going, wrapped in strange, unfamiliar packages. They are for you to discover — those messages hidden within. Know you are supported. Notice beauty. Notice joy. Notice the helpful coincidences. Notice the goose bumps or that shiver down your spine when something is true — the tiredness or queasy stomach when you are scared to take a risk. Learn when your body is saying, "No. Don't do it!" When your soul screams that you are heading in the wrong direction. Notice when it feels like the Universe keeps turning up the heat under your feet and asking you to move.

Honor the knowing. The signs are always there. Pay attention. Open your eyes and your heart. Be grateful for each sign as it appears. Take action — a small step in the direction of the sign. Don't ask, "How?" Just do what you know this moment and watch for the next sign — the next coincidence — the next impulse. Follow your truth with love. Let the signs lead you.

~~~

"There's no such thing as chance; And what seems to us merest accident springs from the deepest source of destiny." — Friedrich Schiller

~~~

After the ducks' appearance at my mom's funeral I started thinking about signs and synchronicities. The more I slipped into the energy of listening to The Voice, doing my meditation, and living in the present moment as though it were perfect, the more support and guidance I began to receive and notice. I can look back and find many times when I asked for signs and guidance long before I started writing this book.

In 1998, I was in a slump. I hadn't had an acting audition in weeks and hadn't booked a job in a long while. I was discouraged and ready to give up. I said, "God I'll do anything you want me to do here — you just have to give me a clue. I'll go feed starving children in Africa, if that's what you want. You just have to guide me. What is it I am supposed to be doing?" The next day I got a call from my agent to audition for a new TV show. My agent said, "You are auditioning to be a firefighter. It's the lead in a new segment of a reality re-enactment show." So it wasn't E.R. or one of the other hot TV shows at the time, but it was an audition. My agent gave me the casting director's name and location.

The next afternoon, I walked into the casting office and found the door with the casting director's name on it and signed in. It was only then that I looked at the name of the television show—"It's a Miracle!" I did my first reading with the casting director and was asked to wait in the hall. This was a good sign. They don't ask you to wait if they hate you. Over the next hour, I got called back into the room to read several times with different actors and at the end of it was handed directions to the shoot that would be held the following week. My long dry spell was broken with a show called *It's a Miracle*, which was dedicated to showing real life miracles in people's lives.

Part of me said it was just a coincidence and a fun story to tell. Another part was awed by how quickly I got a response to my question. I continued acting for a couple of more years. Life continued on. I moved from acting to writing plays to studying hypnotherapy—all based on subtle signs and knowing it was time to explore something different in my life. (And now I wonder if that *It's a Miracle* show wasn't pointing to this very path of spiritual awareness that I am walking now.)

In December of 2003, I was questioning whether it might be time to give up my hypnotherapy practice and go back to work full-time in law firms. My client base had grown but wasn't growing fast enough. I didn't feel like I was helping people enough. Was I good at what I was doing? Was this what I was supposed to be doing? My finances were a mess. (This was before the bankruptcy I described in Chapter 2.) I was scared and tired. I said a prayer, "Help me—I need a sign. Should I just fold the business and go back to a full-time management job?" A full-time job with benefits would have a reliable income, but it felt like a step backward. The next morning I went to my office, and there was a package on the doorstep. I opened the small box and in it was a ceramic commuter mug with a note from a former client whom I hadn't seen in over a year. In the note she said, "I don't think I ever told you how much you helped me. I am so grateful for the work you do! I'm so lucky to have found you!" This was a client who came for three sessions and then disappeared and didn't return my phone calls. I had convinced myself that the reason she hadn't called back was about me—that I had done something—that I wasn't good enough. I sat with that note and cried. Why today of all days when I was in my deepest doubt about my practice did that note and gift show up?

The signs came fast and furious when I started writing. It seemed like I'd ask a question, have a need or doubt and the answer was right there. For example, I started questioning the process of how the sacred part of the book was coming to me in my journaling and automatic writings. I said to myself, "I'm kidding myself that anyone could write a book this way." That was Friday. On Sunday there was an article in the *New York Times* about Louise Hay and Hay House Publishing and in it one of my favorite teachers, Wayne Dyer, described writing his books using automatic writing "by hand and without an outline." Dyer said, "I have written them by just letting it come. . . . I don't know where it comes from.... I am just an instrument, and it keeps flowing."[10] I laughed to myself, *Good enough for Wayne, good enough for me.* I guess I had the answer to my question.

Then, several months later, I knew I needed some support and assistance with writing the book. I had

---

[10] Mark Oppenheimer, "The Queen of New Age," *The New York Times Magazine*, May 4, 2008.

notebooks of longhand writing and three-ring binders of typed material—I just didn't know if what I had would hold together as a book. I sat down and said—"God I don't know what I'm doing—help me." The following week I was in a meeting about planning my business goals for the following year and two people down from me at the table was a woman who introduced herself as Ellen Snortland, author of the book *Beauty Bites Beast*,[11] columnist for The *Pasadena Weekly*, performer and book coach. Not only was the help I asked for sitting in the same room with me but she was someone whose column had made me laugh and made me think. I introduced myself to her. I told her that her recommendation of taking a full-impact self-defense class in her column had helped me greatly with my fears after 9/11 and the elevator incident after my deposition. Taking that self-defense class had empowered me and changed my life; not just in learning physical skills to protect myself but in learning great boundary setting skills As I thanked her for the work she did, I looked at her and she had tears in her eyes. She said, "Sometimes you wonder if what you do really matters. Thank you." So, one day I said I needed support with this book; the following week, I met Ellen. I got to reinforce for her how important her work was when she needed it. I also found a godmother/book coach and a writer's group who helped me shape the chapters for this book.

In the time surrounding my mother's death, there were so many signs and synchronicities, like the songs that played

---

[11] Ellen B. Snortland, *Beauty Bites Beast: Awakening the Warrior Within Women and Girls*, B3 Books; 2d edition (August 2001).

on the radio while I was holding vigil. I had been regularly showing up and listening to The Voice for over two years. Things had shifted from feeling like something odd that happened when I sat down with my journal to something normal that I counted on to be there when I needed it. I felt more confident getting quiet and listening. The Voice was familiar enough that I could hear it without stopping to get out my journal. I just needed to check in and ask for the message. A chapter of my life was closing and I needed to make another shift and I wasn't sure what it was. I asked for assistance in determining the next step. Little did I know my life was about to go to the birds.

A mourning dove took up a nest in my backyard cooing away in its plaintive call. I was reminded of sitting on the porch swing between Grandpa and my dad, so little that my feet barely hung off the edge of the swing with my little white Mary Jane's with the tooling in the toes staring back at me while Dad and Grandpa mimicked the calls of the mourning doves. "Whoo, whoo, whoo, whoo, whoo." I remembered feeling safe, surrounded by two men who loved me and would do anything to make sure I was taken care of. A client came to my house and she told me that a mourning dove had been sitting on my front porch when she walked up. "It was the oddest thing," she said, "I thought it was injured and when I walked up, it just flew away." I told her how mourning doves reminded me that my father and grandfather were near. I sensed that I was getting encouragement and comfort from the other side to make those next steps in my life. I knew that I needed to stay with the process of writing that had gotten me this far. And I started contemplating leaving my job at the law firm.

I got home after 2 a.m. one night in July 2010 after working a shift at the law firm and took Sadie out to the front yard for her last "potty" of the night. As I walked back to my front door and stepped onto the porch something started to fly above my head circling tightly between my porch light and mailbox. I ducked because I thought it was a bat — but when I looked up it was a blue jay. I didn't think blue jays were nocturnal. What the heck was it with the birds? I entered the house and went to the Internet and looked up *blue jay medicine*. Blue jays meant that it was time to embrace my talents and embrace life to the fullest pursuing what I loved. One site even said, "Use the higher knowledge that you get from the spiritual realms to make good things happen for you here on earth."[12] Once again I got that little chill of "truth bumps."

Part of me thought all these messages were for the birds — they were superstition and coincidence. But a greater part deep inside knew the ring of truth in those messages. It was time. I could either admit that my life and the way I saw the world had been forever changed or I could ignore the depth and beauty of my connection to The Voice and the signs being sent my way. I noticed that these bird encounters were warming my heart. I was connected to something sacred, something bigger than me that was asking me to be more.

The signs and synchronicities are gifts of hope and faith. When I ask for guidance with an open heart, I am no longer surprised at the signs that show up. Maybe they are always there but when I ask, I am opening my eyes to collecting that

---

[12] http://blog.peacockandpaisley.com/bluejay-symbolism/2008/09/08/

evidence. When I see with the eyes of love, there are indeed miracles unfolding right before my eyes. I say, "Thank You!" as I connect with ease and flow from a loving and benevolent Universe. As I step into this flow, I see more synchronicities. I feel sacred and interwoven with all of life.

Are you aware of the signs and synchronicities around you? Do you say "thank you" when you encounter them?

CHAPTER 17

LEAP! YOU DON'T NEED A NET

You came here to experience life and yet you hold back. You get by. You survive. You keep waiting for the time to be perfect. You keep waiting till you have no fear. You kept trying to plan for all possibilities. You think that you are staying safe but you are only wasting time. Your life will be over in a blink and then you'll see all the wondrous options you had. You'll wish you could choose again.

If today isn't a good day for you to live sacred — when is? If the economy scares you, if your obligations overwhelm you, it is because you are running your life on reduced power — not from the greater connection of the sacred. You are stuck in the human, not your beautiful divine self.

Fear sees the impermanence of life and makes you freeze or run away. Sacred sees the impermanence of life and gives you courage and compassion to move forward. Do you want to live a life rich with experiences or a safe life untouched and unchallenged? Do not twist yourself up in what is logical. Follow your heart and let your mind serve your loving vision. Enter the age of miracles.

Take the hero's journey. Have courage. Be bold. Live your life now. No excuses. Trust that I wouldn't be urging you to fly if you couldn't. Leap in faith and love. There is no cliff — no net — because you do not need a net. You can fly. You have the wings I gave you. They are tucked away behind fearful expectations but they are there and will carry you to beautiful heights if you let them. Spread your wings, open your heart and fly. Fear will melt away as you say yes. I am the air currents that support your flight. I tell you this because you are ready. It is time.

~~~

"Security is mostly a superstition. It does not exist in nature, nor do the children of men as a whole experience it. Avoiding danger is no safer in the long run than outright exposure. Life is either a daring adventure, or nothing."

—Helen Keller

~~~

Throughout the time I have been writing this book, I keep getting this message over and over again: *"Leap! It is time."* And I'd say to myself, "Time for what? Leap where?" *"Into the sacred,"* The Voice would say. I had taken many leaps that others called brave—from stepping down as manager to pursue my acting dream to jumping out of an airplane.

I didn't know how to leap into the sacred. I felt beauty when I was connected to The Voice but there seemed to be a lot more pressure to follow what the other voices of fear were saying. "Be practical, pay the rent. People don't live by the whispers of some weird Voice inside that you are probably making up anyway." I would take small steps that would move me from scared to not-so-scared but I wasn't making it to sacred.

My whole life I've heard the saying, "Leap and the net will appear." That phrase is about trusting that the Universe will provide and help you when you take action toward a goal. When you move forward in faith and take a leap, there will be support that you didn't imagine or anticipate. I know this to be true. But I've stopped saying this phrase to myself because "leap and the net will appear" focuses on needing a net, because I might fail. And when I focus on failure I probably will—like the time I almost drowned in four feet of water that I could stand in because I was focusing on how I didn't swim well when my college friends threw me in a lake.

There is a cartoon that I saw years ago and it stuck in my mind. It is a picture of two birds sitting on the limb of a tree. One bird has a parachute pack on his back and the other bird is saying, "Your trouble is that you lack self-confidence!" Just like that bird, many of us forget our natural talents and we forget the support of spirit and friends. I know there have been so many times when opportunities have come up and I have not taken the leap because I felt that I wasn't ready or didn't know how it was going to work. The trouble is we can never learn to fly or be what we were called to be by playing it safe like the bird wearing a parachute. We have to take leaps to prove to ourselves how capable and supported we are.

In July 2008, a friend loaned me $5,000 so that I could focus on writing and not have to work at the law firm. The plan was that I would pay her back from my 401(k) once I had left the firm. But once the money was in my hand, I didn't trust enough to actually leave the firm. I kept postponing my departure waiting for the right time. I couldn't completely let go and trust that this was something I was supposed to do and that Spirit was supporting it through a helpful friend. I used part of the money to supplement my income so I didn't have to work as many hours. I was embarrassed that I hadn't taken the leap and felt uncomfortable around my friend. What was supposed to be a short term loan was stretching out. Even though I had countless signs of how much spirit was supporting me as I worked on this project, I kept telling myself that it wasn't logical or practical to leave. The mind can be crafty in creating reasons why you can't do something that your heart calls you to do. Practical sounds good until you realize that you can connect with the miraculous instead. It took me another two years to get ready to leap.

A week or so after my mother's death, I called employee benefits to see about taking money from my 401(k) to help pay for Mom's funeral expenses and the person on the other end of the phone said that I'd have to show that it was a hardship and that I had exhausted all other measures including applying for a loan to pay for the funeral. My blood pressure shot up. The firm had no loan provisions in their plan and now with over $100,000 in the account, and a $12,000 funeral expense that I needed at least $6000 to pay my half of the expenses, they were telling me I needed to take out a loan from a bank instead of having access to my own money. I had no business taking out a loan. I thought to myself, "If I quit, you'll have to give me all my money." And the light bulb went off. If I quit, they have to give me the money. This is what I was going to do two years before — quit and finish this book.

My logical mind jumped in and asked, "How is that supposed to work? You've taken two years out from building your hypnotherapy practice to write. You only have a handful of clients. You don't have a book deal yet. Tell me, what are you planning to do?" And as much as my logical mind tried to tell me it wasn't a smart move to leave the law firm, the quieter part said, "Leap!" I knew I probably would never make any progress unless I took the leap. Staying at the law firm was like I was trying to swim across a lake but holding onto the pier and wondering why I wasn't getting anywhere.

The Voice said, *"Let it go, you'll succeed beyond your wildest imaginings if you just trust and let go."* I wanted to. I really wanted to. But I still was uncertain. My scared self needed some hand holding. I talked to a life coach friend whom I can count on to help me know whether it is spirit or fear talking. She, of course, told me to leap. I went to talk to a financial planner, expecting him to tell me to stay at the law firm job and to lecture me about tax consequences of tapping into my 401(k). Instead, we had an amazing discussion about faith, taking a leap and how hard it is to grow a business while working a job. (And yes, we had the practical discussion about money, too!) One of my more financially conservative friends who has always asked me if I was certain about what I wanted to do said, "I think it is time to take your message to the world." Another friend told me her guides told her to tell me that I was a writer and I should be teaching small groups of people the messages of this book. But the thing that capped it for me was small and simple. I walked into the New Alexandria Bookstore in Pasadena to buy a birthday gift for a friend and my eyes were drawn to a colorful poster on the wall. The colors were perfect for my living room so I moved closer to see exactly what the art was. I laughed as I looked at it and its message by Margaret Shepherd, "Sometimes your only available transportation is a leap of faith." I bought the poster and knew there was no way I could make any other decision.

So in the midst of an uncertain economy, with only a couple of months worth of money in cash and a 401(k) as backup, I walked into the law firm administrator's office and gave notice. My ego and fear were screaming, "What the hell are you doing?" And to be honest I wasn't sure how it was all going to work. I just knew it was time. I needed to see if The Voice was right. Did I have wings?

My last day at the law firm was sweet and sad. I had worked there longer than I had lived in my parent's home. It was a family of sorts—and perhaps like all families, a bit dysfunctional. I had truly grown up there. One of the partners wrote me an email and said that he couldn't imagine the firm without me, that I had taught him to work the copy machine many years before in his first week as a summer associate. I was touched by the support from my peers, all of whom cheered me on. So many people told me I was brave to take the risk. I didn't feel brave. Part of me was still terrified but I knew that if I wasn't willing to fully claim my life now, I might never do it. I walked out the door of the law firm with a bag holding the relics of twenty-one years of work, and walked into my new life.

I didn't know exactly what that new life was going to be or how it was going to work, but I was ready to leap, unfold the wings I had kept hidden and see if I could fly. It was almost like I could hear The Voice breathing a sigh of relief, *She's on her way.*

I wasn't sure where I was going other than listening and following The Voice's direction. I was scared but I felt like I was moving closer to sacred. I had no idea exactly where the journey would take me. Part of being sacred is how we hold uncertainty as simply something that hasn't been revealed yet rather than something to fear. I knew I needed to do this more than anything else I had done in my life. It was time to follow my heart and the Sacred Voice within, trusting that I would be guided to where I needed to go next, trusting that my wings would unfold.

Are you holding onto something that no longer serves you and trying to create something new? Are you getting messages that it is time to take a leap of faith? Are you being asked to trust your wings?

CHAPTER 18

SURRENDERING TO MY BECOMING

It's not about work, love. It is about life. Your soul purpose is not your job. It is the blossoming of you. Step in. Step in. Continue to step in. Forget about what's next and how it is going to work. Live now. Trust that the whole universe supports your growth and evolution. Let go and surrender to living. I will lead you to the next moment. Live from your heart and soul. Let your spirit join your humanness in this beautiful dance called life.

Each day remember who you are. Your heart knows. You are the meeting of heaven and earth. You are the spirit that takes form. You are the sacred embodied in the world in this momentary unique expression. Honor your light. See and be gentle with your darkness. Own your experience of the never ending evolution of you and the evolution of the world. You are growing into an expansive version of yourself that only your spirit has the blueprint for.

You will never create a life with your mind and muscle that is more magical and amazing than the one you will create with your heart and spirit in full trust and surrender of the whispers of your soul. Sit in your essential self which is timeless. Only by listening to your heart and soul will you fulfill your purpose here. There is no one else on your exact journey. You can't judge how you are doing by comparing yourself to anyone else.

Fully participate. Share what you hear — your power, your talents and gifts for the good of all. Take the next step in consciousness as it reveals itself to you. Fully enjoy and participate in the now.

Being sacred is not passive or tentative. Great visions are not achieved without bold action. Your courageous heart already has the key to your becoming. Have faith in the journey that is life itself. Fully express who you are as you become more you. That is enough. Relax and move with the flow of consciousness. Give thanks for the unfolding. You are exactly where you are supposed to be — surrender — let go, enjoy the ride. Embrace the sacred in you. Embrace the unseen, the unspoken — the things known about — not of the mind but of the heart. Listen. You've heard the whispers before. Connect now and live the Mystery.

~~~

"If you surrender completely to the moments as they pass, you live more richly those moments."
— Anne Morrow Lindbergh

~~~

In the days after I left the law firm, I traded my part-time job for a full-time ego driven need to complete this book in the next three months. In retrospect, it was a little arrogant to put myself on deadline to understand enough about the sacred so that I could have a completed manuscript. As the days progressed, the more I tried to wrap it up in a neat package, the more lost I felt. I struggled with trying to come up with the grand conclusion so that I could say, "TA-Dah! I'm complete." It wasn't going to be that easy. Every time I'd show up to write, a panicked part of me would say, "I don't know. I don't have the answers. How am I supposed to complete this book?"

"If you want me to write about being sacred, you are going to have to help me here," I said to the powers behind The Voice, still secretly hoping for quick inspiration to finish the book. Instead, I heard, *"Take the class."* I knew immediately that The Voice was talking about "Healing the Light Body," a seven-week certification course in energy medicine taught by the Four Winds Society. The program is based on healing methods of shamanic traditions in South America combined with information from science and psychology more tailored for the Western mind. Each time I came across the brochure, there was a longing that was beyond the intellectual need to take another class to add another tool to my practice. For over seven years, the course had come in and out of my awareness. I'd find the brochure or a mention of it on the Internet. One of my clients told me she was taking the program. She invited me to take part in a healing ceremony with some visiting shamans from Peru. I loved every experience I had of the material from the program, but when it came to taking the class, I had many reasons why the timing wasn't right.

Instead, I read books by Alberto Villoldo, founder of The Four Winds Society. His description of the feminine energies of the Divine in shamanistic traditions aligned with what The Voice whispered to me every day.

"[I]n the more ancient, feminine theologies, we were never expelled from the garden or separated from God. . . . We actually participate with the divine in the co-creation of our Universe. We recognize that everything in our world is sacred, including us, and that our job is to foster the fullest expression of that divinity"[13]

"Everything in our world is a miracle. Everything is sacred. There is nothing that is not," whispered in my brain again and again.

As much as I wanted to take the program, I hesitated. Signing up for seven weeks of classes over the next year would put me behind in completing the book and building my business. *"Your life is not a book. There is no ahead or behind; there is only now and how you choose to use it. Follow your heart. Surrender outcome,"* The Voice said. I walked out on the ledge of faith, took a deep breath and tapped into my 401(k) money to pay for the classes.

I traveled to Park City, Utah to take my first class in September 2010. Riding the shared ride shuttle from Salt Lake City to Park City, I found myself seated next to Bettie, a writer working for a major Internet company who lived less than ten miles from my house in Los Angeles. She was going to Park City to take the Four Winds class, too. We didn't really know what the experience was going to entail, but we were excited to begin. We talked and laughed our way up the mountain. By the time we arrived at our hotel, I felt like a kid who had found her first friend at camp.

---

[13] Alberto Villodo, *The Four Insights, Wisdom, Power and Grace of the Earthkeepers*, Introduction pp. xv-xvi, ©2006, Hay House, Inc., Carlsbad, CA. Reprinted with permission.

The class was comprised of approximately 22 people from all walks of life, including two physicians. As I sat with these amazing people, I felt like I had found a lost tribe and had walked this path many times in the past. I heard the language of the spirit of my heart being spoken. Honor nature and every being, align with the highest for all, dream a new world into being, and create new stories of love, peace and empowerment. I learned hands-on healing techniques that surprised me in their power and effectiveness. Standing around the fire at an evening fire ceremony, I felt connected to the lineage of people across time that had circled around a fire in community and ceremony.

The phrase "stepping into your becoming" was used over and over again in class. This phrase helped me have words for what I had been experiencing since I said yes to listening to this Voice and writing about this journey. I wasn't going to reach a final destination called sacred. I was stepping into the next phase of my own unfolding in sacred consciousness. Where our lives and paths will take us is uncertain and the more we try to know, the more anxious we become. We are never done and exactly what will happen next is a mystery. The sacred connection already exists, we just have to remember it again and again. We choose how we see—everything as interconnected, deserving of love and honor, sacred, or everything as separate, where we have to be on our guard and be scared.

This sacred dance between my efforts, how I show up in the world and when I let go and allow the highest powers of the universe to work, has been tricky to master. My ego likes to maintain an illusion of control and having things figured out. I have the same tendency in working with Spirit as I do when I ballroom dance. I don't trust my partner to lead me. I'm sure it is annoying for the guy trying to dance with me and I'm certain the greater spirit within looks out from my heart and sighs, "There she goes again trying to figure it all out when she could simply relax, let it flow from me." It has been in the times when I've given up and asked the Universe to lead me that things have flowed the easiest in my life. But it seems I keep getting to that surrender by exhausting myself.

Being in the moment is that phrase that we have all heard so many times from so many teachers. I see another beautiful parallel between my acting training and how I am supposed to live in real life. When I studied acting, there was preparation needed to perform a play or shoot a scene. I had to learn my lines and create a background story for the character to give those words texture and meaning. I had to learn my blocking (stage or film choreography—where do I go when?). But when it came time to perform, I needed to trust the preparation enough to let it all go and just be present in the moment with the other actors in the scene and allow the scene to unfold. It took me a long time to find out how much preparation I needed in order to be able to throw it all away and be spontaneous within the actual performance. As a novice actor, I wanted to have every move all figured out in advance. It made for a very dull performance. But once I had the experience of how good it felt to be flying by the seat of my pants in the amazing experience of being in the flow, I never wanted to go back to the plodding way that I approached scenes when I first started acting. There were magical surprises, and it was so much fun doing the work.

So, too, it is tricky to know when I need to take action and when I am pushing too hard trying to force something to happen. The better route is to surrender and abandon the judgment of right and wrong, of being "there" or "not there yet," and live in the certainty that being in this moment is enough.

Life isn't a test. It is an opportunity for our spirits to experience our humanness in this wonderful dance we call life! It is a continual dance of becoming — not a destination. It has taken me a lifetime (maybe many lifetimes) to come to this point, where I can listen and step forward into unknown, the mystery, the connection and let the beauty of it take my breath away. There is no destination named "sacred" but there is a magical journey of choosing to be led by the highest connection within. When we do this we are at our most sacred. It is a reclaiming and a rediscovery of what is already there. We remember and we forget. We come in and out of the dance with that part of ourselves. Fortunately, our spirits are very forgiving partners; they always welcome us back to the dance with open arms.

As I look at the world today with all its fast moving changes, great shifts, challenges, and perhaps even chaos, I can let the uncertainty drive me to fear or reaffirm my connection to my soul's journey. It is a dance of owning who I am and what I know, and admitting I don't know anything at the same time. It is embracing a new way of viewing myself, the world and everything in it. It is seeing things in the world that scare me, accepting that fear is part of the human experience, then choosing to let the higher energy within me run my life.

While I thought my mission was a job that I needed to find or this book to finish, it isn't. My mission is simply my unfolding in sacredness — showing up with love, doing what I was called to do in the moment and letting the rest go. It isn't passive. It is alert, aware and fully present. It is partnering with the Divine in the sacred dance of creation, which is life itself.

We are all looking for ways to be happier, to be connected to life, to understand why we are here. We can't find that in any book or in any class, we can only find that in developing a true relationship with all the aspects of ourselves. As we embrace how complicated, we are, we can accept the same complexity in others. When we can honor the continual dance that each of us is dancing, we step closer and closer to the sacred.

I'm not at a place where I live consciously in the sacred 100% of the time. Maybe there are few people who are so enlightened walking amongst us, but they are not in my personal acquaintance and probably not in yours. We all have moments where we forget that connection. I get triggered. I find myself being catty. When I find my fear leading the way, I remind myself to surrender and invite my spirit to lead me again. I have learned to stop judging myself for feeling fear and instead, start loving myself through those fears. I coax the scared part to take one step forward in the direction of my dreams and rejoin the dance of becoming. I've found that the soul's path is seldom the most comfortable path but it is the one that makes you feel most alive.

Sometimes I do this gracefully, other times I take some hard falls. It's all part of living. I tune into The Voice and ask it to share with me. I step into the dance called life with gratitude, lightness, joy and laughter in my heart. It is a magical dance. Its unfolding continues to surprise and delight me. I am in communion with life and every being on the planet and I am so thankful.

> **Are you ready to accept that you are constantly becoming? Can you trust that? What are you being asked to do by your higher voice? How have you been able to learn to dance with spirit? Each calling of your heart is an opportunity to continue getting closer and closer to the essential you of your being in this moment.**

A Note to Readers

Committing to listen to the spirit voice journey has completely changed my life, my relationship with myself and my connection to others. This journey is a process of constant evolution. There is no "there" to get to. There are moments that signal to you that the old fears that used to stop you are no longer doing so. One of those moments for me was leaving the safe world of the law firm and following my heart to study with the Four Winds. In those moments, I surrendered to the idea of living in the unfolding and not knowing where the journey would take me. I have to say life has only gotten more amazing as I listen to the Voice Within and I wouldn't have it any other way. Stepping onto the healer/shaman path has fit like no other career before because it is a way of being not just my job.

I hope my stories inspire or comfort you as you find your own spirit dance. Spirit isn't something out there away from us, it lives within. I invite you to explore, reclaim or deepen the connection to the sacred within you. Find a practice that helps you tune into your own highest Voice or knowing.

The daily journaling practice was how I learned to tune the radio and check with The Voice, my higher self and its guidance. My practice might not work for you, but if you ask to be guided to what works for you, with an open heart, I know you will find it. Develop a practice of noticing the dance of your humanness and your spirit, the scared and the sacred. That is why we are here in this amazing gift called life.

All along I've been encouraging you to look at your stories. If you answered the questions at the end of each chapter you have somewhere to begin. Are the stories helpful to you or should you shift them and let them go? Each story we tell defines how we move forward. Crafting my story for you made me realize that it is actually as we tell our stories that we are determining the trajectory of our lives.

One of my goals in releasing this book was to spark a new discussion about what living sacred means and how we support each other in our becoming. For me, living sacred means choosing to let love and the highest whispers of my spirit run the show. If we all chose to let the highest whispers of our spirits guide us to our becoming, what kind of world would we create? The dream of that is stunning. I don't know what the critical mass of people is that tips a world view. But I do know that this becoming is already happening. Have you already heard whispers? Are you living by their guidance? Are you confused about how to make this a regular practice?

Spirit keeps giving me "good stuff" to share. The Voice said we had many books to write and I can't wait to find out what I will learn as the dance continues.

You can connect with me on Twitter (@scaredtosacred), Facebook (www.facebook.com/Carolwoodliffauthor) and at Carolwoodliff.com. Stop by and join in a discussion. I'd love to hear from you.

ACKNOWLEDGMENTS

& DEEPEST GRATITUDE

Because I believe great writers and thinkers deserve credit, I've done my best to source the quotes I have used. Any error here is unintentional. Thank you to all who inspired me and helped me illustrate my points with their beautiful words.

SOURCES MENTIONED AND QUOTED:

CHAPTER 1

Page 10, Quote by Eleanor Roosevelt from Eleanor Roosevelt, *You Learn by Living,* Harper; 1st edition (1960) p. 29 – 30.

CHAPTER 2

Page 18, Quote by Mary Pickford from Mary Pickford, *Why Not Try God?,* Chapter 6 (newspaper serial), appeared in *St. Petersburg Times,* 25 January 1936, sect. 2, p. 3.

Page 18, Pierre Teilhard de Chardin, *Le Phénomene Humain,* (Originally Published in French) ©1955 Editions du Seuil, Paris. English translation *The Phenomenon of Man* by Bernard Wall and introduction by Julian Huxley, ©1959 William Collins Sons & Co. Ltd., London and Harper & Row, Publishers Incorporated, New York.

Page 21, Quote by Thomas Merton from Thomas Merton, *No Man is An Island* ©1955 The Abbey of Our Lady of Gethsemani, renewed

1983 trustees of the Merton Legacy Trust, Shambhala Publications 2005, page 134.

Page 23, Chellie Campbell, *The Wealthy Spirit, Daily Affirmations for Financial Stress Reduction*, ©2002 Chellie Campbell, Sourcebooks, Inc, Naperville, IL. (Great book to put you in a better money mindset.)

CHAPTER 3

Page 28, Galileo quote: Letter to the Grand Duchess Christina (1615), in response to enquiries of Christina of Tuscany, as quoted in *Aspects of Western Civilization: Problems and Sources in History* (1988) by Perry McAdow Rogers, p. 53.

CHAPTER 4

Page 36, Albert Einstein quote. William Hermanns, *Einstein and the Poet: In Search of the Cosmic Man,* ©1983 Branden Books, Page 16.

CHAPTER 5

Page 44, quote from Osho, *Zen Tarot The Transcendental Game of Zen,* ©1994 Osho International Foundation, St. Martin's Press, New York. Pg 54. [The credits in this book say that the commentary is based on notes by the illustrator Deva Padma. So I'm giving both OSHO and Deva Padma credit for the quote.]

Pages 47-48, lyrics from "Hold On" by Marty Casey ©2006 Martin Casey, Bob John Kourelis, Dino John Kourelis, William C. Sawilchik. Thank you to Lovehammers, Marty, Bobby, Dino, and Billy for bringing me back to myself and reminding me that play is essential to well-being. If you love rock 'n' roll, check them out at www.lovehammers.com.

CHAPTER 6

Page 54, Golda Meir quote from Golda Meir Interview with Oriana Fallaci published in *Ms.* magazine (April 1973).

CHAPTER 7

Page 66, Emerson quote from Ralph Waldo Emerson 1841 Essay on Friendship reprinted in *Three Centuries of American Poetry and Prose* edited by Alphonso Gerald Newcomer, Alice Ebba Andrews, Howard Judson Hall, ©1917 Scott Foreman & Company, page 427. Found on Google books at http://books.google.com/books?id=JwcuAAAAYAAJ&dq.

Page 68, Julia Cameron, *The Artist's Way, A Spiritual Path to Higher Creativity*, ©1992, 2002 Julia Cameron, Jeremy P. Tarcher/Putnam.

CHAPTER 8

Page 74, Benjamin Frankin quote from *Poor Richard's Almanac*, 1746.

CHAPTER 9

Page 80, Pema Chödrön quote from Pema Chödrön, *When Things Falls Apart Heart Advice for Difficult Times*, ©1997 Pema Chödrön, page 12.

CHAPTER 10

Page 90, Wayne Dyer Quote. On his PBS special on *The Power of Intention*, Wayne Dyer shared this quote saying that he had heard it somewhere but could no longer remember the source. See also: Wayne Dyer, *The Power of Intention*, ©2004 Hay House, Carlsbad, CA.

CHAPTER 11

Page 98, Virginia Woolf quote from Virginia Woolf, *The Moment and Other Essays* (Harcourt, Brace, 1948)

Page 99, Lies, Lies, Lies, ©1982 by The Thompson Twins, Thomas Bailey, Alannah Joy Currie, and Joseph Martin Leeway.

CHAPTER 12

Page 108, Lao Tzu, Chinese Philosopher, founder of Taoism, wrote *Tao Te Ching* (also *The Book of the Way*), 600 BC-531 BC.

Page 111, Lyrics from: "Watch With Me" by Joe Wise, © 1972 by GIA Publications, Inc., 7404 S. Mason Ave., Chicago, IL 60638 www.giamusic.com, 800.442.1358. All rights reserved. Used by permission. Thank you Joe Wise for writing a song that reminded me of what was most important in my mother's final days.

CHAPTER 13

Page 116, Elisabeth Kübler-Ross quote from Elisabeth Kübler-Ross: Messenger of Love, by Lennie Kronisch, *Yoga Journal*, November-1976, page 19.

CHAPTER 14

Page 124, Rainer Maria Rilke quote from *Letters to a Young Poet*, letter dated August 12, 1904.

CHAPTER 15

Page 132, Kahlil Gibran quote from Kahlil Gibran, *The Prophet* 1923

CHAPTER 16

Page 146, Friedrich Schiller, *Wallenstein* (1798) Part II Wallensteins Tod (The Death of Wallenstein) Act II, sc. iii (Translated by Samuel Taylor Coleridge)

Page 148, Quote by Wayne Dwyer from Mark Oppenheimer, "The Queen of New Age," *The New York Times Magazine*, May 4, 2008.

Page 149, Ellen B. Snortland, *Beauty Bites Beast: Awakening the Warrior Within Women and Girls*, ©2001 B3 Books; 2d edition.

CHAPTER 17

Page 154, Helen Keller quote from Helen Keller, *The Open Door* © 1957, Doubleday.

CHAPTER 18

Page 162, Anne Morrow Lindbergh quote, from Anne Morrow Lindbergh, *Bring Me a Unicorn: Diaries and Letters of Anne Morrow Lindbergh, 1922-1928,* ©1971, 1972 Anne Morrow Lindbergh, Harcourt Inc ed. 1993, page 120.

Page 164, Excerpt from Alberto Villoldo, *The Four Insights, Wisdom, Power and Grace of the Earthkeepers,* by Alberto Villoldo ©2006, Hay House, Inc., Carlsbad, CA. All rights reserved. Reprinted by permission. Thank you to Alberto Villoldo for your wisdom & inspiration!

THANKS TO FAMILY, FRIENDS AND SUPPORTERS:

To my sister Luanne thanks for going first and making my firsts easier. Thanks for looking out for Mom when I was so far away. Love to you, Rachel, Sean & Rebecca. Always in my heart.

Karen Maleck-Whiteley—dear friend and sister of my heart—without you saying, "You don't have a choice—you have to write," and support, this book would never have been completed.

Ellen Snortland and Lisa Gaeta, Pauline Field, Alaine Lowell, Dianne Williams, Louise Yount, Tim Burgess and all my Writer's Workout friends who helped give feedback and shape this book.

Dear friends who encouraged me, read, commented, and proofread: Anna Stookey, Connie Eakes, Dana Taylor, Darci Fersch, Elizabeth Decker, Felicia Sutphen, Gail Ross, Joanne Sprott, Jon Powell, Julie Barrier, Julie Cowell, Kathleen Fealy, Kimberly Barclay, Kristi Toia, Laurice Brown, Lynn Gilman, Margaret Prietto, Michael Hui, Michelle Hubastek, Miriam Siryam, Nicole D'Andrea, Noelle Brown, Sally Sterling, Scott Rothman, Stephanie Bettman, and Susan Kay Wyatt. It truly did take a village of support to complete this book and I'm so lucky you are in mine!

To Arna Vodenos for all your wisdom, mentoring and support, for sharing your heart and helping me grow in spirit.

To Anita Jesse, wise acting teacher & dear friend: the things I learned with you in acting class continue to inform my life each and every day.

To my tribe at the Four Winds Society, my courage to be transparent comes from the work I've done in my classes and ceremonies with you.

Robert Evans, James Twyman and Randy Davila for the Next Top Spiritual Author Contest, and Christine Kloser and The Transformational Author Experience. You created "contests" that weren't contests at all, but ways for authors all around the world to connect. I'm blessed by the knowledge you shared and the friends you brought into my life.

To all the wise authors who have inspired me and helped form who I am today as a writer and spiritual explorer on this earth, especially: Julie Cameron, Chellie Campbell, Pema Chödrön, Deepak Chopra, Sonia Choquette, Wayne Dyer, Elizabeth Gilbert, Louise Hay, Anne Lamott, Caroline Myss, Eckhart Tolle, Alberto Villoldo, Neil Donald Walsch, and Marianne Williamson.

To my clients, it is a joy to work with you and see you find the wings of your amazing hearts and spirits. You honor me with your trust. Thank you for teaching me each session more about this beautiful spirit dance we call life.

To those readers of this book, who read all the way to the end including these acknowledgments. Thank you for sharing my journey. Bless you all!

Abundant thanks to the Universe for allowing me to hear those whispers and supporting me through this process. To that most holy power of love and light that fuels us all — Thank you, Thank you, Thank you!

With deepest love,

Carol

ABOUT THE COVER ILLUSTRATOR

I was so fortunate that spirit connected me with the amazing artist Annie b. who heard me describe my vision for the cover of this book and then created something even better than I imagined.

Annie b. lives in Cornwall, England with her husband and son. She has developed her own unique style and language, in oils, watercolors and chalk pastels. Beginning with a meditation and tuning into her angelic guides, then allowing the colors to blend and flow, and the magic (healing) to shine through onto the canvas. Annie b. also paints personalized Guardian Angel, Spiritual and Soul Connection Portraits, by commission.

Annie states "My aim is to create artwork that helps us all feel love and joy, see the bigger picture and the natural flow of life so that we all may dance in harmony together, be mindful of mother earth and each other, and know the Divine Oneness we truly are."

Thank you Annie. You are a gift!

To learn more about Annie b. visit www.annieb-art.co.uk.

ABOUT THE AUTHOR

Carol Woodliff is a Western Shaman, intuitive coach and speaker based in Los Angeles, California. She is passionate about helping people be gentle and loving with their human selves while taking this spirit journey we call life.

Carol is sought after by other healers and transformational leaders for her ability to identify and help release energetic blocks that have been resistant to change. Carol holds a safe loving space to release chronic pain, trauma, deeply held emotions and stories that keep clients settling for less than who they know they are.

She is certified as a Healing the Light Body Practitioner by The Four Winds Society, A Reiki Master, a Hypnotherapist and a grounded mystic who lives connected to the Voice that guided her to write this book while fully embracing all the ups and downs of being human. She loves writing, photography, travel and her amazing spirit teacher dog, Sadie. Learn more about her at her website: http://carolwoodliff.com. Connect with her on Facebook at www.Facebook.com/CarolWoodliffauthor.

Printed in Great Britain
by Amazon

28547388R00108